RENEWING THE JOYS OF TEACHING

RENEWING THE JOYS OF TEACHING

How the Principles of Stoicism Can Return Fulfillment to the Classroom

JOSEPH GRAVES

ROWMAN & LITTLEFIELD
Lanham • Boulder • New York • London

Published by Rowman & Littlefield
An imprint of The Rowman & Littlefield Publishing Group, Inc.
4501 Forbes Boulevard, Suite 200, Lanham, Maryland 20706
www.rowman.com

86-90 Paul Street, London EC2A 4NE

British Library Cataloguing in Publication Information Available

Library of Congress Cataloging-in-Publication Data
Names: Graves, Joseph (Superintendent), author.
  Title: Renewing the joys of teaching : How the principles of stoicism can return fulfillment to the classroom / Joseph Graves.
  Description: Lanham : Rowman & Littlefield, [2023] | Summary: "This book applies the various principles of Stoicism, as explicated by these founders, practitioners, and evangelists, to the realities of modern life, particularly as lived by educators-teachers, principals, para-educators, and all of the others who toil in schools-post Covid"-- Provided by publisher.
  Identifiers: LCCN 2022061723 (print) | LCCN 2022061724 (ebook) | ISBN 9781475872286 (cloth) | ISBN 9781475872293 (paperback) | ISBN 9781475872309 (ebook)
  Subjects: LCSH: Teaching--Philosophy. | Teachers--Psychology. | Stoics.
  Classification: LCC LB1025.3 .G734 2023 (print) | LCC LB1025.3 (ebook) | DDC 370.15--dc23/eng/20230210
  LC record available at https://lccn.loc.gov/2022061723
  LC ebook record available at https://lccn.loc.gov/2022061724

♾️™ The paper used in this publication meets the minimum requirements of American National Standard for Information Sciences—Permanence of Paper for Printed Library Materials, ANSI/ NISO Z39.48-1992.

For Cheryl

CONTENTS

Preface

The last three years have been difficult for those of us working in schools. In March of 2020, the governor of my state recommended that, in the face of a pandemic of unclear severity, we close our schools. Like every other school superintendent in South Dakota, I did precisely that. The result was an entire quarter of the school year lost to learning. Oh, we all did our best to send home packets, teach virtually, and employ every other weapon in our instructional armament, but even as we did so, we knew were fighting a losing battle. We were quickly surrendering hard-won ground.

If you had ever told me that closing schools nine weeks early would be a time of anxiety and stress, I would have laughed out loud. But that is exactly what it was. For the first time in my career (then spanning over thirty years), I didn't enjoy going to work. The teachers were working from home. The paraeducators were gone; the buses, motionless. Worst of all, the students were home, and the virtual education program we had set up for them, while fairly sophisticated, just wasn't doing the trick. As with summer break—when students from middle- and upper-class backgrounds either hold steady or even advance and those from families of a lower socioeconomic status regress—the same discouraging reality unfolded. And this time we could watch it live on the footage broadcast from hundreds of cameras. It was like watching one of those wildlife documentaries, red in tooth and claw, where the lioness picks off the baby zebra. We were simultaneously horrified and helpless to do anything about it.

Now I am generally a pretty joyful person. I have a loving wife, four wonderful adult children complete with a bevy of grandchildren, and a profession I love. Day-to-day things may make me happy or sad, but I'm almost never truly melancholy, which is why the personal impact of the pandemic's shutdown of schools was a genuine surprise to me. My father, a lifelong educator, used to (laughingly) say after a professional development day, "You know, teaching would be a really great job if it weren't for those damned kids." I still laugh when I think of him saying it. Ironically, though, it turns out the very opposite is true. Education sans kids is a terrible job. I started putting up videos of myself reading to the (virtual) kids from classic children's books in the public domain and imagining their smiling faces as they listened with rapt attention. I knew it was unlikely that many were actually tuning in, but when it's all you've got, you go with it. Certainly, the number sitting in their basements playing video games vastly outnumbered those tuning in to my rendition of *The Jungle Book.*

As the fourth quarter finally expired—a lost opportunity of the worst kind—summer began. It didn't help. Yes, it was summer, and usually, though I work year-round, the tasks are different enough that it feels like a break of sorts. The problem was that I kept dwelling on the fact that I hadn't earned it. By the third week of August, when our school year begins (our governor was one of the first to order schools re-opened), I was ecstatic that we could finally put the school closure behind us and return to a normal school year. Yeah, right—it wasn't normal at all. We had a mask mandate for all personnel and students in the building. The Department of Health and our building offices monitored close contacts and sent potentially infected staff and students home by the dozens every day. Classrooms looked like bank teller stations, with transparent shields around every desk. Some parents pulled children out of school, others demanded increasingly draconian measures be taken for student safety, and still others demanded precisely the opposite. Board meetings, which had normally been snooze fests in my district, suddenly erupted into ideological battles. Amid all of the chaos and testing and social distancing, though, there was something more. Something worse. People were growing increasingly miserable, even desperate.

Somehow, we made it through that year. Summer dawned and it was better, at least for me, as I felt I had earned this one. But then it wasn't better. The pandemic continued, lingered, and then ramped up again with all of its variants, one more infectious than the last. The new school year came but with all manner of uncertainties. And now, many in schools simply couldn't go on. Their reserves of happiness, contentment, or mental health were simply overdrawn. Some retired. Others found new professions. The education departments of the nation's colleges and universities saw enrollments shrink. Teacher shortages crashed against school walls, like a tsunami against a third-world shore—so did shortages of school custodians, secretaries, and bus drivers. If a school has a job, that job had a shortage of qualified applicants. Most teachers and other school employees stayed, of course, but very few—perhaps none—without some mark, some lingering side effect, not of COVID but of having worked in schools *during* COVID, its realities and its scares.

This year, 2022–2023, the third since that disastrous quarter of closings in 2020, most schools have reopened and with very little in the way of masks or shields or virus testing materials. The pandemic may or may not have left us, but we have left it.

So *why*, then, are so many teachers and other educators—administrative, certified, and support—still down in the dumps? Who knows for sure?

But the longer it goes on, the longer we continue to pick at each other over offenses, imagined and real, emanating from those 2¼ school years, the more it seems that the condition, the malaise, might be permanent. That teaching and working and serving in schools might not be worth it after all.

I disagree, of course. I chose education as a profession because I felt it was a worthy way to spend my life. The famous psychologist Erik Erikson postulated eight stages of psychosocial development, binary decisions we all must make as we make our way through life. So as an infant, we must choose between trust and mistrust. At life's end, where I seem more and more to find my reality, we choose between integrity and despair. If we find that we've lived our lives well, we enjoy integrity and can enjoy life's golden years. If, however, we find that our lives have been misspent in shallow or meaningless pursuits, a chasm of despair opens before us. So many I see these days strike a frightening resemblance to that despair. For many others, as they abandon a profession they once found meaningful, a worthy task at which they can expend their life's efforts, I fear their exhaustion will lead them to a life's work not worth it, not up to their once (and future) expectations.

I worry for them.

But I don't just worry. I also have what I feel is a solution for many. It can be found in the words and life of the long-dead Roman emperor Marcus Aurelius. It can be found in the teachings of the also long-dead Roman philosophers Seneca and Epictetus, as well as Greek philosopher Zeno of Citium. These were proponents and practitioners of an ancient philosophy called Stoicism.

Now, especially to all English teachers out there, Stoicism is a different thing entirely from being stoic. Stoicism is a way of life, while being *stoic* is a personality trait—that of being emotionally undemonstrative. The two have little, if anything, to do with one another. Frankly, whether you are stoic or not is neither here nor there. It doesn't really matter.

Stoicism, however, is a life's philosophy, a carefully considered way of living your life such that you will not just have a life well lived but also one with a regular, even steady, experience of joy, of happiness. In times such as ours, in a profession we all once believed in but so many today are losing faith in, Stoicism may well be a way of finding our way through the angst and pain to a new love of and joy in teaching.

Introduction

This is not a book on academic philosophy, the kind of philosophy taught in America's graduate schools of philosophy. While such studies have immense value, they tend to be long in theory and critical analysis and short—or virtually absent—on application. This, then, is not the book to pick up in order to garner an academic mastery of an ancient school of philosophy or deeply explore the biographies of Greek and Roman philosophers.

Thus, neither of these will happen within these pages. They won't, because modern philosophies and modern critiques of ancient (or just past) philosophical schools have become so abstract, so filled with pedantic vocabulary, so completely divorced from any connection to life as it is lived, as to be irrelevant and incomprehensible for the vast majority of people. Oddly, a graduate school of philosophy in any university in the West would be the very last place to look for someone seeking out a life philosophy to guide them to truth or meaning. It cannot be found there.

Nevertheless, there once was a time when schools of philosophy did provide such guidance, such perspectives on life. Socrates was no pedant. He was a man who argued in the streets of Athens and called people to better, clearer understandings of life and the world around them. He would have never earned his PhD (yes, that's an anachronism), because he never wrote anything down, though he did leave a note for one of his students to settle a debt of a chicken after his imminent death.

These schools of philosophy not only provided a lamp for their students on how best to live their lives but even competed with one another to attract students and hold sway in the marketplace of ideas. It is one of the things that makes Greece (largely Athens) and her cultural heir,

Rome, unique in the evolution of Western civilization. Philosophies were neither arcane fields of study that turned on impenetrable vocabulary nor sophist arguments aimed at winning the day rather than identifying the truth.

Most educated people have at least heard of some of these schools: Epicureanism, Cynicism, Skepticism, and, of course Stoicism. This is actually part of the problem. Each of these schools has lent its name to a personality trait, but much of the meaning of the underlying words have lost their meaning in the transmutation. Matt Groening's debauched robot in *Futurama* is anything but Epicurean. (Go ahead, look it up, he's hilarious.) Cynics are not necessarily cynical. Skeptics not all that skeptical. And true Stoics may appear to be stoical, but this is mainly because of the ancient devotion to *gravitas*, the outward manifestations of the seriousness of life, rather than the demands of Stoicism.

In order to clarify just what Stoics believed then and believe today, chapter 1 will be devoted to just that: a review of the principles of Stoicism. It can be a bit esoteric at times, but it is also fundamental to understanding this philosophy and how it can potentially deliver educators from the current malaise. Chapter 2 is a quick review of some of the most important and most famous Stoics of ancient Greece and Rome. This chapter is less critical, and the reader can skip it if they wish. Then again, you'll find a Roman emperor there—remember Marcus Aurelius from *The Gladiator*? You'll also find a couple of iconic heroes, whose lives progress very much in the line of all Greek heroes in their theater.

The rest of the book, beginning with chapter 3, applies the various principles of Stoicism, as explicated by these founders, practitioners, and evangelists, to the realities of modern life, particularly as lived by educators—teachers, principals, paraeducators, and all of the others who toil in schools—post-COVID. As such, the remaining chapters aren't really dependent upon one another and so can be consumed in any order the reader chooses. Regardless, each attempts to provide the reader with Stoic tools and techniques that will enhance their life and, especially, their professional happiness. For, as Marcus Aurelius has offered, "The happiness of your life depends upon the quality of your thoughts."[1]

The appendix can be read by those interested in the implications of Stoicism for Christians, on the one hand, and atheists, on the other, especially those concerned that that this philosophical school would interfere with either.

NOTE

1. Marcus Aurelius, Meditations, book III, chapter IX.

CHAPTER I

The Essence of Stoicism

IN THE INTRODUCTION, IT WAS MADE CLEAR THAT STOICISM IS A VERY different thing than being stoic. Stoic people are unexpressive with neither a smile nor a frown on their face. Think of the depictions of the ancient Greeks, those busts that grace bookshelves, or even of the American founding fathers, all displaying that sense of gravitas. Life is a serious business, and no Caesar or Cincinnatus, Washington or Jefferson, were going to stray from that reality by depictions of themselves with emotional displays, positive or negative. If *any* emotion emanates from those marble statues and paintings, it would be sternness.

The same is true of those ancient Greeks and Romans who pursued a life's philosophy of Stoicism, even though their lives as they lived them were filled with joy and tranquility. For that was the goal of Stoicism—*to live a good life.* (Stoicism, from its beginnings with Zeno of Citium, actually had three main areas of interest: logic, physics, and ethics, but only that last topic, properly understood, will be explored in this book.)

That *properly understood* phrase might seem like a dodge, but it's really not. Rather, it is necessary because "moderns" have all kinds of different understandings of what makes a good life. Endless consumerism; sexual pleasure; eighteen holes of golf, seven days a week; world travel; owning the latest technology; eating the finest foods; diving deeply into alcohol and drugs; installing home theaters with virtually infinite entertainment offerings; honing one's body to physical perfection; gaining fame—the list goes on and on. But pursuing any of these without reflection puts the cart before the horse. Stoicism, instead, starts at first principles—or at least earlier principles—sort of the way geometry starts with postulates about points and lines.

The following are Stoicism's postulates:

1. Living life well requires one to live in accordance with nature.

2. Living in accordance with nature means living as human beings were *designed* to live.

Thus, for example, Stoicism understands human beings to be social creatures. This means people have duties to others—to treat them justly, to care for them, and to provide for them based upon one's relationship to them. When people meet these obligations, they attain virtue. When they attain virtue, they also attain tranquility, happiness.

Happiness—to belabor the point perhaps too much as the reader, in all likelihood, already understands or intuits—is not the giddiness so evident in a first grade classroom when the students revel in their Halloween party, which so often so quickly devolves into its opposite (as the sugar high kicks in). Rather, happiness is something calmer, deeper, and more permanent. It is largely unaffected by the ups and downs of daily life, the various travails of the classroom, or even the stroke of luck or the odd seeming coincidences of Alexander's . . . *Terrible, Horrible, No Good, Very Bad Day.*

A Stoic would greet both the lottery win and the automobile accident with equal equanimity because neither would truly affect her underlying happiness. For that happiness, developed by living a virtuous life—one that has met its obligations, that is consistent with how a fully human life should be lived—is rooted in deep soil, committed to an understanding of how life should be lived. Bad days have about as much effect on a true Stoic's happiness as losing (or finding, for that matter) a twenty-dollar bill has on Warren Buffet's financial position.

Superficial pursuits—those mentioned above—cannot affect happiness. Almost any person who has lived long at all or learned the vicarious lessons from celebrities and social media personalities *knows* this. Educators have a particularly spectacular view of the full range of the superficial because they spend their days with the young and very young. From the Kindergartner who is inconsolable over the show-and-tell project forgotten at home on the kitchen counter, to the middle schooler's ebullience over a compliment over their clothing choice, to the freshman's despondency over a social group's slight, teachers try to empathize with their pupils' genuinely held feelings while helping them to better understand their importance or lack thereof.

And they see the ramifications of parental decision making upon their students. Those who are granted every whim by parents and who live unconstrained by such "silly" rules as bedtimes, limited television or video games, and nutritional guidelines find themselves unhappy, even though they so often get precisely what they want. Alternatively, those who have their basic needs met while asked to live within reasonable constraints are generally happy.

Well, the same is true of adults. The difference is that those who have reached the age of majority have to set their own restraints, having left behind the bonds of their benevolent parents. Adults must set their own vision, their own philosophy of life, and then map out the best way to get there.

And that best way to get there, according to the Stoics, is through the virtuous life. Depending upon the Stoic referenced, four virtues embody such a life: courage, wisdom, restraint, and justice. First, notice what's not included: winning, wealth, fame, or personal "success"—which is not to say that the ancient Greek and Roman stoics were devoid of these things. Seneca was one of the wealthiest men of his day; Cato, a successful political activist; and Marcus Aurelius, a Roman emperor, for Pete's sake. And all of them were Stoics. But these successes, though not scorned by them, were not central to their happiness, except inasmuch as they were manifestations of one or more of these virtues.

Thus, it is time to talk about these four virtues.

COURAGE

Courage, Aristotle (who was not a Stoic) said, could be found between the traits of cowardice and foolhardiness.[1] Aristotle's *golden mean* technique can be incredibly useful, though it is not directly on point in a discussion of Stoicism, except that finding and facing the truth is critical in pursuit of it. For the Stoic, courage or bravery is meeting one's obligations to others; remaining true to Stoic principles, especially never flinching from being fully human and all that requires; not accepting untruths; and accepting with a clear mind the vicissitudes of life even unto death.

Epictetus notes the rather high demand this places on the Stoic when he writes (in his *Fragments*, a collection of his adages gathered from various original sources), "It is much more necessary to cure the soul than the body; for death is better than a bad life."[2] This is not an argument for euthanasia for a bad life as referred to *here* means to live one's life poorly, in error—not to live with illness.

Living up to this Stoic version of the virtue of courage, caveat emptor, can be a daunting undertaking. Cato, fighting for the Roman Republic rather than tyranny at the hands of emperors, died not for his sins but for his virtues. Yet Cato and Stoics in general would argue that even though he was murdered, abandonment of his principles would have led to an unhappy life, while abiding by them led to a happy, though abbreviated, one.

Currently in education, a great deal of ink is being spilt on critical race theory (CRT). CRT refers to teaching history and social issues as if the only determining factor in any of them is race. This is analogous to Karl Marx's sense of economic determinism, that all of history and human behavior can be explained by materialist (i.e., stuff and money) factors, and the social classes that result. For Marx, it's all about socio-economic class. For CRT, it's all about race. While race is historically important, it's not the whole megillah.

Aristotle's golden mean can be fruitfully brought to bear here as well. To find the proper way to teach history and current events, look between the two opposing ideologies. CRT, in the left column, argues that history is nothing but a transcription of interactions, largely exploitative, between the races. In the right column is the notion that race is irrelevant to history. To accept this latter idea is to engage in or accept *revisionist history*, one stunning example of which is the *lost cause* interpretation of the American Civil War. This is the idea that the war was fought for reasons entirely other than slavery.

It was the rather astonishingly successful public relations effort of ex-Confederates and southern sympathizers to paint the Civil War as the 'war between the states' or the 'war of Northern aggression.' Partisans of this view, an attempt to lift the blame for the war and its more than six hundred thousand deaths from the southern states, argue that the war was not to protect slavery but, rather, to protect state's right or defend southern soil from northern invaders. (As Shelby Foote, in one of his characteristic witticisms, describes a Confederate soldier's response to a Union soldier as to why he was fighting, "I'm fighting because you're down here."[3])

To find the appropriate way to teach history, including the causes of the Civil War, the teacher must look between CRT and the revisionist history of the lost cause. Betwixt them can be found the correct position that race does have an impact on historical events, but it is not the *only* factor that is relevant. That middle position calls the teacher to look at historical events with an unflinching eye; to take a cold, hard, and candid look; and to teach the truth. Telling school-aged children they are somehow responsible for the oppressions of other races in the past is as foolish and inaccurate as is whitewashing history of the obvious racial inputs to so many tragedies of the past.

That is, in fact, the Stoic position. It is possible—in fact, many have done it—to just go along with CRT. It is possible—tens of millions utilized it as a salve for their guilt over a war that not only cost them a generation of their young men but was fought for a deeply unjust cause—to assert the lost cause. But both are lies, and the fact that it might be easier to accept or modify one's behavior or teaching to avoid conflict with those who offer those lies leaves one living "ill."

Teaching the Civil War faithfully is only one example of displaying Stoic courage in the classroom. For others, this poses different demands. Some teachers today are concerned about an overemphasis on technology. They see their school's one-to-one computer initiative as exacerbating children's overexposure to screens. Why put yet another screen in front of second graders in the classroom when perhaps a book would be a better option? Maybe it's the de-emphasis on teaching cursive writing or phonics, when the research on both demonstrates quite clearly their value. Or what should one make of homework? Various researchers are arguing for its value, others for its lack thereof. Teachers and principals who become convinced of the research basis for or against homework and reasonably believe it is genuinely in the best interest of children cannot simply ignore this reality. Rather, they must face that reality, to fight for it, if they are to meet their obligations to their students. Doing otherwise lacks courage.

Doing so, however, past the point of making a difference (depending on the importance), may not be a matter of courage. It may, instead, be a matter of wisdom or a lack thereof.

WISDOM

Wisdom, for the Stoics, consists of knowing the difference between good, evil, and neither good nor evil, as well as clearly understanding the difference between things they can and cannot control.

"You have power over your mind—not outside events. Realize this, and you will find strength."[4]

This idea is not, of course, exclusive to the Stoics. One of its more popular manifestations is, in fact, found in the Serenity Prayer, probably written by twentieth-century American theologian Reinhold Niebuhr. The salient portion of that prayer reads as follows: "God grant me the serenity to accept the things I cannot change, courage to change the things I can, and the wisdom to know the difference."[5]

Historical Stoics, preceding Niebuhr by more than two thousand years, would agree, and in fact, many of them were religious men in their own right, though appealing to a different pantheon. In other cases, they accepted simply a nature of reality. Regardless, Stoics argued strongly that advocating for or fighting against that which is out of one's control is a fool's errand. Worse, it interferes with one's happiness, causing people to become ineffectually upset or expend time, energy, and resources for things that are unattainable, immutable. Far better to work toward ends that are under one's control, and it is these things which are the true opportunity cost—that which we give up when we spend resources in other ways—of misguided efforts.

For many years in schools, an inspirational poster called for students to never give up. To illustrate the point, a frog, which was firmly crammed into a heron's gullet, stretched out its arms to grasp its predator around the throat so it could not swallow. Giving up—or not trying in the first place—can indeed be a ticket to failure, especially if it becomes a habit. Thus, giving up *is* a bad idea—except when it's not. To the hard-nosed view of reality of the Stoic, giving up or not pursuing a cause in the first place is not necessarily bad. If the matter is outside of one's control, it is the only sensible decision. The efforts and time and talent wasted on tilting at such windmills would be far better spent, far more effectively spent, on those things that can be controlled.

One of the quickest ways for a teacher to find unhappiness in his career is by railing endlessly against things he cannot control. Take the case of an elementary school teacher with a room full of spirited pupils. One of his eight-year-olds, Jace, struggles to learn and produces subpar work because he cannot stay awake in class. As the teacher engages with the child, he discovers that Jace's parents allow him to play video games well into the wee hours of the morning. He's read the research. He knows that elementary-aged children often need eight to ten hours of sleep a night. Teenagers can require even more. So he schedules a meeting with the parents and diplomatically raises the issue of bedtimes (or, in the case of a high school student, of their "part-time" work schedules.) The parents are quick to assure him that they give their third grader an 8:00 p.m. bedtime and scrupulously enforce it, or they throw up their hands and signal that truly sad omen of parental surrender, "I try to do that, but he just won't listen. I can't make him!"

Don't misunderstand. The Stoic philosophy isn't telling this teacher to butt out. A good teacher has an obligation to others, and that obligation is a steep one when it comes to his students. He needs to take every reasonable step to convince or help the parent find a way to fix their child's sleep cycle. In the end, though, a teacher is not the child's parent. They've identified the solution but now need to understand that is an area they cannot ultimately control. Teachers who keep banging their head against this wall even when it separates their students from greater success in the classroom will neither succeed nor achieve tranquility.

They must separate the controllable from the uncontrollable, to give each student the best experience possible for the seven-hour day or the fifty-to-ninety-minute class period (in the case of the teenager) when they have them each day—and then move on. Trying to control what you cannot control is foolish. Understanding the difference and accepting that is wisdom. In wisdom is happiness.

In the modern world, it is not just prayers that agree with the Stoic Emperor. So did that great American philosopher Yogi Berra, who offered his own view on control and happiness. "There are lots of things you can't control, but how you respond to those things is the one thing you can control."[6]

RESTRAINT

Sometimes called temperance, restraint identifies what is essential and limits itself to it. This requires the Stoic to neither accept less than he needs (or others need) nor to grasp for more. "Busy yourself with but few things," says the philosopher, "if you would be tranquil." But consider if it would not be better to say, "Do what is necessary."[7]

Zeno of Citium lived this out in his lifestyle, finding tranquility in having and pursuing very little in the way of food and drink, dress, and possessions. Zeno's, though, was only one approach. Later Stoics would argue—and live this out—that such wealth and those things that accompany it were not inconsistent with their philosophy as long as they felt no attachment to them. More on this later. What truly brings unhappiness and a lack of tranquility are commitment to and grasping for material goods beyond those that are necessary to sustain life. Zeno felt the siren song for stuff was just too strong. Other Stoics—Marcus Aurelius and Seneca are two excellent examples—felt it was possible to own many possessions without those possessions owning them.

Consider the case of a school superintendent who sometimes (though less than one might think) finds himself at odds with employee unions/associations. He is in this unhappy place, in part, because he believes some of them contribute to their members' unhappiness, and he wants people to be happy in their profession. Associations or unions exist to secure an increasingly enhanced compensation package and work conditions for their members. One of the truths about being happy with one's work is satisfaction (pay never brings happiness, except in the very, very short-term) with their pay. One of the unfortunate realities in America is the perception among educators that they are dismally paid. It's a perception deeply rooted in the American experience. Since Ichabod Crane rode the backroads of Sleepy Hollow in search of food and lodging with the families of his students as much of his compensation, the schoolmaster's path has not been one ending in prosperity. Following the Second World War, those who led classrooms were typically earning significantly lower wages than the industrial or line workers who shared in the economic boom and American economic dominance of that era. In the 1950s and 1960s, in Sioux Falls, South Dakota, as one example, teacher pay was really quite poor. Sioux Falls, like many American cities, was heavily dependent on a single industrial employer, John Morrell & Company, a large pork and beef slaughterhouse. Morrell's employees, easily the plurality among workers in that community, were well compensated with high hourly wages, generous insurance coverage, and an enviable pension plan. Teachers made far less than these industrial workers, even though the training requirements for educators were much higher. This was true in many cities and states in America.

That has changed. Today, teachers are paid much better. Unfortunately, that perception seems to not be shared by most educators. School administrators and teachers continue to lament their compensation level, never even stopping to acknowledge that their paychecks are a lot fatter than they used to be. So are educators today adequately paid? Well, teachers, guidance counselors, principals, and other certified employees certainly earn enough to live a middle-class lifestyle, providing much more than just the necessities of life.

Yet there is always a sense in the profession that educators don't make enough, that the value of the job—which is enormous—does not match the pay stub, that the pay for educators is less, often far less, than those in professions that seemingly contribute far less to the common good. Why does the man who can hit a baseball, the vapid starlet, the endlessly bickering member of Congress, or the investment banker make far more, sometimes hundreds or thousands of times more, than the money a teacher does? The actual answer, of course, is that is how capitalism works. But the answer matters less than the question. Comparing personal compensation with those of others, typically a game of cherry-picking anyway, is a sure ticket to unhappiness. The Stoic says to be happy with less. And the same result can be reached with "Be happy with your pay." Asking how a teacher's pay compares with someone else's will almost always leave the questioner unhappy. Asking if one's pay is enough, if adopting the Stoic commitment to less, will do the opposite.

And it isn't just the teachers.

A group of school superintendents in a midwestern state met together quarterly to discuss issues, share solutions, and set legislative positions for education. One of the means of communication was an e-mail group, which allowed them to send out concise questions, requesting fresh ideas. Then one year, one of the superintendents—very much not a Stoic—asked the others to provide their salary amount, 403(b) contribution percentage, school car provisions, and benefit packages—all the way down to whether they were offered an annual, free medical checkup. Most responded, though some grudgingly. After the first year, it became an annual information request, and it became clear that this educational CEO was using the data received, triangulating it with enrollment data and job responsibilities, as ammunition for his annual raise from his school board. (Two years later, incidentally, he lost his job, suggesting that this was not ultimately an effective means of negotiating his compensation package. More importantly, though, it was clear that his constant measurements and comparisons were making him miserable.) Any lag in his compensation *in any category* left him spitting mad over the unfairness, and this was someone paid *well above* the average. If the purpose of life and especially one's professional life is to maximize income, his strategy made sense (until, that is, he got fired), but if the purpose of life is tranquility, deep-seated joy, then it was completely counterproductive. He traded away happiness for money, something no Stoic would do.

There is, of course, a point where too little income brings unhappiness. But once enough income is incoming—providing the basics of life (i.e., food, housing, clothing)—expending efforts to earn more will not enhance happiness. In fact, it will actually detract from it. The political capital and effort expended in pursuit of more will actually drain the underlying reservoir of joy.

But that might just be an unpersuasive example and one unlikely to make one inclined toward Stoicism. Instead, then, consider curriculum bloat. Some school districts, some states, and even some countries—France has traditionally been an excellent example—are highly prescriptive about curriculum and lesson plans. Others offer teachers a great deal of autonomy. Their state DOE (department of education) or board of education or legislature issues the state standards for each curriculum area and says, "OK, now you figure how best to teach them." And even schools and states with detailed instructions on what and how to teach are fooling themselves in many ways. Face it, when the teacher steps into their classroom and quietly shuts their door behind them, they are the master. The elementary teachers, principals used to quip, 'are the queens of their realms.'

Within certain limits, an instructor teaches what they want, how long they want, and the way they want. This is a good chunk of what makes teaching a profession—or an enterprise always reaching for that brass ring—that is, autonomy based on expertise. Once dissatisfaction with pay has been eliminated, a lot of being happy with their life's work as a professional is the degree of autonomy found in the job. The vast majority of teachers and principals and paraeducators and other school employees want to have significant decision-making authority in their workspace. And they should.

This is particularly important when it comes to the curriculum. To put it as bluntly as possible, schools are being asked to teach far more today than in the past but also far more than they can possibly teach in a seven-hour school day and a 180-day calendar.

Consider the experience of the hapless first-year teacher—in this case, one cutting his teeth in world history in the mid-1980s. His first year (and this was when there was thirty years less to teach!), the school year came crashing to an end in the middle of his unit on the Industrial Revolution. Yup, he never even made it to the twentieth century, when the most relevant content was found—what an unmitigated disaster. Yet it happened because he took the curriculum and state standards and textbook seriously, even scrupulously. He faithfully covered every topic in every historical era until he ran out of time before he ran out of history. The result was that he left out the most important material. What he should have done, instead (and in his defense, he did this the second year he taught the class), was map the curriculum, notice it couldn't all be taught, and then cover all of the most essential items and delete (with loud lamentation but a clear conscience) those of lesser importance. He needed to grasp the *necessary* and limit himself to it. Thank you, Emperor. (By the way, he still covered Marcus Aurelius.)

All teachers are in the same boat. The third-grade teacher beating herself up over the fact that she's been given the impossible task of teaching everything that the standards or the district curriculum guides say she must teach needs to stop it. Instead, she needs to cut either the nonessentials or the least essential, teach the rest thoroughly and with regard to actual student mastery rather than just coverage, and then smile. At the elementary level, this probably means giving lots of time to literacy and numeracy, while trimming back on social studies or science (or, better, integrating them into reading and math instruction). That is a shame, but the former are essential and the latter, less so. That doesn't mean they are unimportant, just less important than getting children up to their reading levels.

The Stoic virtue of temperance also speaks to the balance between family and school. Teachers and school administrators, in particular, must remember that they have obligations, not just to their students but to all those in their life. Consider, again, that group of post–World War II teachers. Their pay was so poor that they often took second jobs or found ways to enhance their compensation within the school. This generation, remembering the Great Depression of their childhoods, went to school at 6:30 a.m., taught all day, and coached three sports after school. The only moderating factor was this was at a time when the majority of mothers still worked solely in the home. Children were ridiculously well cared for by their mothers, and so the system worked. Today, with most couples, both work outside the home, and many others are single parents. This *can be* a recipe for disaster for personal and family life. The profession of education cannot be reasonably calling upon its practitioners to sacrifice the upbringing of their own children in the call to raise the children of others. That old canard about no one on their death bed ever wishing they had spent more time at the office is just too schmaltzy, but it does contain an important kernel of truth. Don't limit your sense of essential, the essence of appropriately exercising restraint, to work life.

JUSTICE

As with the word *stoic* itself, justice and its connotations can easily lead people astray as they attempt to understand Stoicism. Marcus Aurelius believed—and his writings support this, as he covered the topic more fully than any other—that justice was "the source of all the other virtues."[8] Without it, in other words, all else was lost. He defined justice socially, as doing right by others but in ascending layers, from those within the household to one's entire society.

He argues essentially for mutual interdependence, that people are so completely intertwined with others of their species that anything done to boost the happiness or satisfaction of others will inevitably reflect its rays and benefits back upon those who offered that justice in the first place. Likewise, anything that detracts from the joy of others, even if intended to bring benefit to the actor, will inevitably lower his own experience of joy. He even argues, quite persuasively, that a large portion of the human being's *raison d'être* is doing good for others. He sums up this view, sometimes originally ascribed to Gaius Musonius Rufus, by saying, "What injures the hive injures the bee."[9]

This is, in a very real sense, a comparatively easy one for educators who tend to be, after all, 'people's people.' But this is not the norm. In private enterprise, for example, trade secrets are carefully safeguarded, and there is a clear distinction between us and them—those people inside the company with whom other employees cooperate and work as a team and those people from other companies with whom they compete for customers and profits. Consider that perennial Yuletide classic movie *A Miracle on 34th Street*. In it, Kris Kringle, presumed to be just the Macy's department store Santa Claus, points out to children and parents the availability of sought-after toys and even better prices on specific toys at competitor's stores. The executives are aghast (until they realize it is a wonderful marketing ploy). The standard practice is to only recommend Macy's toys at Macy's prices. Normally, to do what Kris is doing is tantamount to mercantile treason. Try watching this movie with an executive in retail business, and gauge their first reaction to Macy's wayward Santa. (But stick with the 1947 film, not its remakes.)

Then watch the movie with other teachers. They'll get the joke about a privately employed Santa encouraging people to shop elsewhere, but they won't really *appreciate* it. They won't, because that's not how things are done in education, definitely not in public but also not in private schools as well. Teachers routinely share new techniques and instructional materials with other teachers. It is a point of amusement among educators that there is no such thing as an original idea. Even the most innovative of practitioners, it is widely believed, just stole their ideas from somebody else. In fact, one of the strongest arguments against merit pay for teachers is just that: it will create endless, harmful competition among people who should be working together for a common good.

For this reason, a relative lack of competition in education, the concept of Stoic justice does have less of an impact on educators. But less doesn't mean none, and in fact, there are some important consequences of a focus on justice as an important Stoic virtue for those working in schools. The COVID pandemic was a definite crisis in schools. As noted in the introduction, schools closed to in-person instruction, required masks, mandated vaccinations, and took any number of other actions designed to minimize the spread of the virus. In some cases, educators and political leaders focused so intently on the pandemic as a public health issue that they de-emphasized the reality of it as an educational crisis. The result, according to the National Assessment of Educational Progress and myriad other educational research organizations, has been a student achievement disaster. Remembering that the Stoic virtue of courage requires an unflinching facing of the truth, and while education should not bear all the blame for such, it must acknowledge its share. At times—in different places and among different individuals—educators put their own sense of safety and even fear ahead of the impacts they frankly knew or had to know they would have on students. And the kids suffered.

Another outcome of this reality has been a marked increase in American students attending private schools and home schools. That isn't necessarily a negative—legal, respectful competition can be helpful to all parties—but most public education advocates lament the fact. It is a demonstration of the results of acting unjustly, in the Stoic sense. Fail to act justly toward others—in this case, allowing students to wither on the vine—and the fruits of those injustices will be visited upon everyone.

Ok, that's the macro level, and it's one with very little in the way of personal implications or lessons. But there are others. One would be the area of teacher mentoring. Though the education departments of colleges and universities today are light-years ahead of the reality of even a few decades ago, it remains true that the most important time of any teacher's career is year one. In this they are a bit like the loggerhead sea turtle. When the hatchling finds its way out of the sand-covered nest, those first yards it faces between nest and surf are the most perilous. Exposed to predators, with streetlights leading them astray (i.e., away from the water), and exposed to any number of other environmental threats, they succeed or fail on those few meters of beach.

So it is with the new teacher. The workload, because their instructional briefcase is all but bare; the disciplinary challenges, because their bag of tricks for responding to such is shallow and untried, are many; and the parental engagements, because their own experience in school was probably as a teacher pleaser, can be overwhelming. According to much of the research, the success of such new teachers is greatly boosted by the presence of a skilled mentor. This is someone who can give them ideas for dealing with that resistant child, the outrageous demands of parents, the shortcuts for lesson planning, and even the need to find time for a personal life (to the extent there is one that rookie year). But too often, principals and colleague teachers take a more hands-off attitude, feeling that they are themselves overwhelmed or even arguing that they had to walk through the first year's fire and so should the newbie. But when they do this, they further drain the increasingly shallow pool of teachers in the profession. Some even say they don't see a problem with teacher shortages, as it boosts the value of those who remain, maybe even boosting compensation levels. That might even be true.

But it harms the profession. It harms the educational community. Even if it did somehow benefit more senior educators as individuals, it violates the Stoic virtue of justice. To be clear, this is not the same thing as Karma. Karma, the popular notion that what goes around comes around, or that when we do kind things, kindness will inevitably come back to us, and vice versa is not a Stoic concept. Rather, when human beings acknowledge their shared experience in the world, they become just, they act justly, and they become better and ultimately more joyful people. It is personal self-improvement and the understanding that justice benefits everyone at all levels that bring joy, not some chit that comes back to the one who acted justly, sought or unsought. Thus, educators who want more joy, who want a more joyful profession, should extend a hand to the new, harried-sometimes-to-the-point-of-exasperation teacher down the hall.

A similar point can be made for the students. One of the lessons many teachers and principals must learn is that their experience as a student is very similar to those of their students. This is a real problem in the profession. Certification requirements, good in many ways but not without their unintended negative consequences, play into this. State departments of education expect, almost without exception, every teacher and administrator who work in schools to have attended a four-year university and to have graduated with something akin to a liberal arts degree. (That some have relaxed that just now is a concession forced upon them by the realities of post-COVID teacher shortages and one that will be renounced when those shortages ease.) This assumption that all teachers must graduate university is part of what led to the unfortunate perception among educators that students who head anywhere but college after high school commencement are failures. Enlightened educators in the 1960s (and seemingly ever since) lamented *tracking*, not because it erected increasingly higher walls for students to have educational options after high school, but in truth, because it didn't allow otherwise bright students to attend college, which is where *all bright students should go*. There was only one way to succeed and other options—the labor market, technical schools, even community colleges—were not an accomplishment but a booby prize.

The educational profession can excuse itself for this bald-faced snobbery to the extent that it did this through a lack of awareness of the other options. Essentially, all teachers and school administrators pursued a single educational track after high school. Thus, ignorance plays a part. But bias, even prejudice, plays a part as well. For more than the last half century, college-bound high school students looked down on their class-mates heading off to the vo-techs (vocational technical schools) after high school. The student whose skills and intelligence are squandered by enrollment in vocational schools is all but a trope in the movies of the second half of the twentieth century. Take a look at the ending of *Stand by Me* for one example. Those heading for college just couldn't imagine that other economic realities and opportunities existed, ones that brought satisfaction to others that an introduction to philosophy or music appreciation class simply did not. When guidance counselors and teachers and principals treat the non-university-bound students askance—and frankly, it is likely this perception shows through to them no matter how hard educators dissemble—it harms those students and the overall web of people in schools. Such students feel belittled, set aside as less important, and unrecognized for their achievements and skill sets. In all of this, such students are treated unjustly.

That injustice and lack of acknowledgment also results, frequently, in lowered expectations for such students—a pervasive, insidious, and harmful reality. And it is a reality. The instant educators start lowering standards—other than when a student's functional level is organically impeded—they detract from such students' expectations and experience. In the last century, this was done out of an abject socioeconomic-status prejudice. This was reprehensible. Rising awareness in the twenty-first century has eliminated much of that socioeconomic bias, but it's not nec-essarily the lowered expectations. The ever-increasing percentages of stu-dent who qualify for IEPs and 504 plans cannot be justified or explained away by changes in the underlying intellectual capacities of students. Rather, they occur because parents and educators see them as solutions. If the student is not making the grade, lower the grade. It is a stupen-dous trick of cognitive dissonance. Given the choice between changing parent, student, or educator behavior by demanding more, teaching more effectively, and being unwilling to accept a tendency to take the easy route *or* changing the belief (that the student has a disability or other flaw that simply doesn't permit higher levels of success), people do what cognitive dissonance theory predicts. They change their belief. Voila, the problem is solved! But it leaves the student hobbled, adding to whatever was causing their poor performance in the first place—an excuse, an acceptance that this is now the upper limit. In a deeply unfortunate consensus of the student, parent, and educator accepting less, the student is treated unjustly.

Justice is a tall order for the Stoic. It demands not justice for themselves or their family or their friends but for everyone. But, ultimately, it is also what brings deep joy and not the tragic realization, even if only dimly, naggingly understood, of having worked in the educational field and having done less, perhaps far less, than could and should have been done for their students, parents, and colleagues.

SUMMARY

The life of the Stoic is one that maximizes joy and minimizes unhappiness. It does so through living one's life consistent with nature, with what it means to be a human. That means living as a human person is designed to live, not pursuing material wealth or fame or power or any of the other ultimately shallow pursuits of the modern age but pursuing courage, wisdom, restraint, and justice as properly understood, as Stoically understood.

By courage, the Stoic means meeting one's obligations to self and others, even when doing so is difficult. It means adhering to the truth and accepting the inevitable vicissitudes of life. By wisdom, the Stoic means a correct, clear understanding of the difference between good and evil and between things that can be controlled and those that cannot. By restraint, the Stoic means emphasizing the essentials and not grasping beyond those things that are ultimately unnecessary in any case. And by justice, the Stoic means accepting the social nature of humanity and the obligations to others that result. Those who act justly towards all find the joy in spending one's life in its pursuit and the tranquility that comes with the resulting lack of regrets.

NOTES

1. Aristotle, *Nicomachean Ethics*, Chapter II.
2. Epictetus, *Fragments* 32.
3. Foote in
Geoffrey Ward, *The Civil War - An Illustrated History*, Knopf, 1990.
4. Marcus Aurelius, *Meditations*, book 4, chapter 3.
5. Niebuhr, Reinhold, Serenity Prayer, 1926.
6. Berra, Yogi, https://www.baseballbible.net/yogi-berra-quotes/.
7. Marcus Aurelius, *Meditations*, book 4, chapter 24.
8. Marcus Aurelius, *Meditations*, book XI, chapter 10.
9. Marcus Aurelius, *Meditations*, book VI, chapter 54.

CHAPTER 2

The Stoics

As noted in the introduction, it is not technically necessary to know much of anything about the great founders, developers, and practitioners of Stoicism in order to understand its precepts. Still, their lives are illustrative of those principles and are useful in refuting some common objections to this school of thought. As this book is intended for educators, some investment in that which is unessential needn't seem gratuitous. In any case, these are condensed versions of what are very interesting lives. As the details of their lives come from fragmentary sources, sometimes written long after the deaths of their subjects and all of their contemporaries, some should be taken with a grain of salt.

Zeno of Citium
Zeno of Citium was a Greek who lived from 336 BC to 265 BC. Zeno, not to be confused with Zeno of Elea (and his famous paradoxes), was the founder of Stoicism. Originally, in fact, his followers were called Zenoians but became known as Stoics because later teachers and practitioners taught in the Stoa Poikile, a covered walkway in Athens. The place name, Stoa, became associated with those teaching there, and thus, they became Stoics. Most philosophy among the Greeks was, in fact, offered in the streets, as opposed to buildings dedicated to their use. Zeno's call to philosophy came after a visit to the Oracle of Delphi. He studied within the Cynic school but could not endure some of its extreme practices, not just bordering on but immersing the Cynic in shamelessness, especially in that far more modest culture than today.

Zeno also rejected Epicureanism, and some see his school very much as a reaction to its focus on pleasure as the greatest goal. He offered virtue and its pathway to tranquility, or inner, real joy, instead. As his school of thought grew in public acclaim, especially among those of political heft and economic means, he was offered Athenian citizenship. This Zeno rejected in part because he was born in Cyprus but also because he did not crave honors (which Athenian citizenship very much was), consistent with Stoic principles. He led an abstemious life, dining on raw food and water, wearing well-used garments far below his economic means, and professing indifference in word and deed to the elements and personal ill health. One account tells of his death from a fall, resulting in a broken toe. In response, he was said to have held his breath, and in so doing, he perished. (There's that "salt" part.) However it happened, in his death, honors showered him, including, much later, the naming of a crater on the moon after him. Thus came immortality, which he, of course, spurned.

SENECA, LUCIUS ANNAEUS, OR SENECA THE YOUNGER

Seneca was a Roman who lived from 4 BC to 65 AD. Seneca was born into a prominent family in what is now Cordoba, Spain. His father, Seneca the Elder, had been a noted teacher of rhetoric in Rome. His older brother met St. Paul the apostle in Achaea in about the year 52 AD (not the last reference to Paul in this book). He was sent with an aunt to Rome for his education, where he excelled in rhetoric and philosophy. Suffering ill health, he moved to Egypt, another Roman province. At around thirty-five years of age, he returned to Rome and became a lawyer and politician. Emperor Caligula determined to execute him for some real or imagined offense but stayed his hand, believing Seneca's poor health would soon finish him off without imperial intervention. Two years later, in 41 AD, he was exiled to Corsica by Emperor Claudius on trumped-up charges of adultery. The emperor's wife convinced her husband to recall him to Rome eight years later, where he became praetor, an office of some authority and distinction, and a tutor to the young Nero. (Imagine having that on one's conscience!) In 62 AD, he retired from public life but continued to write at a feverish pace. In 65 AD, Nero, now emperor, ordered Seneca to commit suicide, rewarding him a rather poor compensation for his work as an educator. Seneca accepted the judgment with equanimity, a most Stoic—in both senses of the word—response. The essentials of Stoicism remained largely unchanged since its founding, though Seneca was an eclectic more than happy to add to or subtract from the overall system as he found concepts consistent with his own sense of reality and justice.

GAIUS MUSONIUS RUFUS

Gaius was a Roman who lived from 20 or 30 AD until no later than 101 AD. The dates of his birth and death are unclear, and much of the rest of his life is similarly ambiguous and disrupted. His school of Stoicism in Rome was well known and well attended. His most famous student was, in fact, Epictetus, and master and student share much of the same philosophical understandings. He was exiled from Rome on at least three different occasions by Nero and Vespasian and possibly others. He was sufficiently well thought of, though, as to escape banishment under Vespasian when, initially, almost all other philosophers—seen increasingly as a threat to the state—were sent away. Musonius either wrote nothing for publication (as with his most famous student) or such has been lost. Two of his other students, Lucius and Pollio, compiled his teachings, resulting in his *Discourses* and another collection that was lost, its existence only known as it is quoted by others. His teachings focused largely on the ethics of Stoicism, viewing the philosophy as the road to a virtuous and thus tranquil life, consistent with following one's (human) nature. He railed against "exposing" children, a form of infanticide practiced by the ancients and argued strongly for an education and training in philosophy for men and women alike. Because of the fragmentary nature of much of his students' writings, Musonius is best known through his preeminent student, Epictetus.

EPICTETUS

Epictetus was a Roman who lived from 55 AD to 135 AD. Unlike Seneca, Epictetus was the child of a female slave, born in Hierapolis in Asia Minor (modern-day Turkey). Epaphroditus, his master, took note of his intellectual gifts and sent him to Rome to study philosophy with

Musonius Rufus. It was something of a status symbol in the Roman world to have a slave highly educated in philosophy. Additionally, Epictetus was unable to engage in much physical labor probably due to a disability from birth. (He is often depicted with a cane.) Around the year 68 AD, Epaphroditus, who had also been a slave eventually freed by Nero in gratitude for revealing an assassination plot again the emperor, went on to emancipate Epictetus in turn. The now free man and gifted student launched his own school in Rome and began teaching Stoic philosophy with great success. In 89 AD, however, the emperor Domitian, growing tired of their antipathy toward autocratic rule and perceived arrogance, banished almost all philosophers from Rome. (Yes, the irony in that is thick.) As a result, Epictetus fled or moved to Nicopolis, Greece, and opened another school, teaching philosophy and developing Stoicism through lectures and lifestyle. Like Socrates and Christ, he wrote nothing down, preferring the spoken word through public lectures to his students and others. One of his students, Flavius Arrianus (a.k.a. Arrian), took copious notes from his lectures and crafted these into eight books, summarizing his master's teaching in the *Enchiridion*. In a subsequent work, *The Discourses,* Arrian reported—verbatim according to him—discussions between the master and his students. (The Greeks and Romans developed any number of techniques for memorization but, even so, the claim to remember such lengthy lectures verbatim seems overblown.) Though a successful teacher with a renowned school of philosophy, Epictetus, consistent with his own Stoic principles, lived a very simple lifestyle and owned very few possessions. Nothing was written as to the cause of his death other than that it was accompanied by universal praise for his life and work. An admirer, in a precursor to modern celebrity culture, even purchased his cheap, earthenware oil lamp for an enormous sum shortly after his death. Epictetus's thought and developments of Stoicism became the guiding intellectual force for Marcus Aurelius.

MARCUS AURELIUS

Marcus Aurelius was a Roman who lived from 121 AD to 180 AD. When Plato espoused the ideal ruler as philosopher king, that seeming archetype was fulfilled in Marcus Aurelius, a man of intellect, upbringing, and devotion to duty. This Roman emperor, the last of those known as the Five Good Emperors, epitomized what Roman citizens viewed as a model ruler. Born to the emperor Hadrian's nephew Marcus Annius Verus and his mother, Domitia Calvilla (from a family of immense wealth), he followed the tortured path of so many of the rulers of the Roman Empire and was adopted by a man who was also adopted by a sitting emperor. From an early age, he studied both philosophy in the Greek fashion as well as the physical arts of wrestling and boxing. His tutors were some of the most prominent scholars and orators in Rome. He continued the Roman adoption of Greek culture (what some would call cultural appropriation today), even penning his *Meditations* in Greek and completing the transfer of Stoicism from Greece to Rome. He was heavily influenced by the thought of Epictetus. His reign was beset with warfare with the Parthian Empire to the east and Germanic tribes to the north. It was, in fact, while he was engaged in a campaign against those latter tribes that he perished, probably from the Antonine Plague, a sweeping illness that resulted in the death of 5 percent of the empire's total population. For those fans of the movie *Gladiator*, his death as portrayed in that movie is entirely fictional. (Commodius was no Marcus Aurelius, but neither was he a psychopathic patricide.) Marcus Aurelius actually ruled with his son, Commodius, beginning in 177 AD. Though he was a popular emperor and an effective one, driving back Rome's enemies and sedulously devoting himself to his duties, he is far better known for his philosophical musings, found mainly in his *Meditations*. To those who argue that Stoicism is a recipe for settling in life, of not achieving great things in life, Caesar Marcus Aurelius Antoninus Augustus is a compelling refutation.

CHAPTER 3

Stoic Skill 1

Negative Visualization

How many funerals pass our houses? Yet we do not think of death. How many untimely deaths? We think only of our son's coming of age, of his service in the army, or of his succession to his father's estate. How many rich men suddenly sink into poverty before our very eyes, without its ever occurring to our minds that our own wealth is exposed to exactly the same risks? When, therefore, misfortune befalls us, we cannot help collapsing all the more completely, because we are struck as it were unawares: a blow which has long been foreseen falls much less heavily upon us.

—SENECA, LETTER TO MARCIA, IX[1]

THE STOICS CAN BE THOUGHT OF AS MANAGERS OF THEIR OWN LIVES. They seek joy through their pursuit of the four virtues discussed in chapter 1. Through the long evolution of their philosophy (lasting at least seven hundred years until its decline after Christianity's recognition as the official religion of the Empire in 380 AD), they also developed a number of skills that, when applied, could manage the various travails of life, which beset the ancients just as they do moderns. Negative visualization is perhaps the skill set with the greatest positive impact on tranquility.

It is the ultimate in proactivity. It has proven so powerful that even some modern cognitive psychologists have adopted it as part of their therapeutic regimens. Marcus Aurelius, Seneca, and Epictetus all wrote at length on its importance. One way to sum it up is, "Well, what's the worst that could happen?" To them, though, this is not a question asked flippantly.

The Stoics were well aware that life situations could turn bad in an instant. Just look at the biographies in chapter 2—plague, physical disabilities, exile, slavery, financial reversals, and orders to commit suicide. If these bogeymen really lurked behind every corner, how could anyone succeed in having an even-keeled, joyful life?

They could do so by taking some time each day or each week for imagining, deeply contemplating, really visualizing, the catastrophes that might befall them. Having imagined the disaster, they could then imagine the way through it. Would it really be so bad? Would it really be as bad as their fevered anxieties might suggest?

Doing this accomplishes two things. First, it helps the visualizer to better appreciate what they have, a challenge for human beings from their inception and one that most certainly continues today. Second, it prepares us for the inevitable. The wit takes note of that fact that human existence is met with one stubbornly unavoidable reality: nobody gets out of it alive. Parents of high school students, when asked if they are worried that they will miss their children when they leave home after graduation, will often reflect that "it really won't be all that different; I never see them anyway." With school, extracurriculars, part-time jobs, and a social life, the little one that had been so ubiquitous in their life has become increasingly a stranger. It is adolescence's way of preparing the parent for an empty (or at least emptying) nest.

Hospice workers report a similar phenomenon with their patients/residents. It is so difficult to leave this life, to contemplate personal death, when life is so good and when they are in the bloom of good health. But when cancer or heart disease or diabetes slowly ramps up pain and nausea, drains energy, and produces malaise, the prospects of death become easier to accept. The manner of approaching death prepares the person for it.

Fortunately (or unfortunately), people cannot always count on life experiences preparing for them for reversals, for losses. Seneca's suicide order and Marcus Aurelius's rapid death from the plague gave neither of them adequate time to naturally prepare. Both were prepared, nevertheless, because they were ardent practitioners of negative visualization. Marcus Aurelius, arguably one of the busiest persons on Earth, took time each and every day to engage in it for the equanimity and tranquility it provided him. But one's personal death is only one—albeit, a particularly crushing one—life experience it assertively addresses.

Take one of the increasingly infrequent minor travails of life, the flat tire (or perhaps the broken chariot wheel?). Earlier generations of drivers dealt with such problems by pulling over and replacing the deflated tire with a spare from the trunk. Today, most drivers are more likely to call a tow service. Either way, it can be exasperating. Imagine the teenaged driver experiencing a flat tire for the first time. In all likelihood, they have no idea how to respond. What they do know is that they are stuck beside the side of the road, calling somebody, anybody, for help. (Imagine the scenario before cell phones!)

One way to deal with such a situation is to train for it ahead of time—learn where to pull a car over, how to use a jack, where to find the spare or at least the donut, and so forth. As the young driver does this, of course, they become familiar with the whole process and discover it's not fun but also not the end of the world. As they visualize it and prepare, some of the venom drains from the bite. Changing a tire is, in the end, a rather simple task, rolling out in a number of sequential, physical steps. Once these are known, it becomes rather easy to handle.

The great Stoics, however, applied this technique to much thornier issues, including death, their own and those of *people they loved.* That latter part may be a bridge too far for some, finding imagining the death of some to be simply too horrible, but the potential devastation of such an experience is also an argument for visualizing just that, for taking at least some of the sting out of such a traumatic event. People who have lost children, for example, never really complete the grieving process. They describe it as becoming part of a club nobody wants to join. Negative visualization can be used for such a horror, but even the great Stoics acknowledged it didn't work completely. Thus, they also marshaled other arguments, including the sense that because a time existed before the deceased and that was not a time of grief, neither should a time after their existence. They also argued, as is still heard today in funeral parlors, that one should expend their efforts in gratitude for the gift of the person's life rather than the loss at their death. One still largely extant example of negative visualization can be found among Roman Catholics and their memento mori (remember death) admonishment. Another less contemporary example may be found among Christian headstones of centuries ago, which cautioned the viewer to do the following:

> "Remember friend as you walk by
> As you are now so once was I
> As I am now you will surely be
> Prepare thyself to follow me."

So why all the talk of death? Other than the fact that it hovers over life in ancient times as well as modern, the great Stoics felt it was effective for even this greatest of life's reversals, its end. But it is hardly the only one, even in the lives of educators. Though career teachers are not as common as they once were, it remains the case that many educators start their career in this profession and end it there, picking up their state pension after decades of loyal service. Many cannot imagine a professional life outside of school.

One particular class of educators is highly susceptible to an involuntary exit from their job, the superintendency. School superintendents, especially in larger districts, have roughly the tenure of the goldfish your daughter won at the carnival ring toss game when she was seven. A favorite adage mentors share with their mentee superintendents is "There are two types of superintendents, those that have been fired . . . and those who *are going* to get fired." Whether any of those mentees really believe it is another question. But what if they did? The truth is that superintendents get fired for any number of reasons. One increasingly common cause is just the changes in school boards, their multiheaded bosses. In as little as one or two years, the board that hired their CEO on the basis of certain priorities to be addressed can shift to a different set of board members with an entirely different—and sometimes even antithetical—set of priorities. After the pandemic passed, some communities, angry over COVID-era restrictions and related issues, threw out board members, electing new ones who promptly threw out their sitting superintendents. It happens.

The resilient superintendent can deal with this reality through negative visualization. Each morning (or once a week or once a month), as she drives to work, she simply imagines a scenario in which a subordinate's embezzlement, an election gone bad, or a crisis not of her making but still demanding a leader take responsibility leads to an involuntary parting of ways. Having done so, she remembers that her professional obligations are less important than those to her family, that no one she loves is dead. She reminds herself that there is a shortage in the field, and so even a termination won't probably be career ending. This causes her to update her resume. She considers other professional opportunities that she could pursue in the event of her contract's termination. After a bit, what looked like a bleak trauma becomes manageable. Unflinchingly facing this fear means that its potential actualization no longer destroys the tranquility in her life now or later.

But superintendents are not the only ones with fears. Teachers enjoy greater job security, but that is not the only specter hiding in their tan, wooden desks at the front of the classroom. What if they fail to use a transgender student's preferred pronoun and become the target of vilification of an advocacy group in their community? What if they determine not to inform a parent of their child's struggles with transgenderism and earn the charge of lying to parents by omission? What if they fail to notice the signs of a student's possible abuse or simply forget to call in the report quickly enough and the child suffers a trauma in the meantime? What if they are the target of a false accusation of inappropriate conduct with one of their students? Teachers spend four years of college and immense time and effort in their preparation for their careers in education. Yet it can all end and be for naught in one unforeseeable incident.

For the Stoic, one great way to address this is precisely to *foresee* it. Pronoun use and parental notification should be matters of school policy.

If the teacher visualizes these as possible scenarios, they can slay those dragons by abiding by that policy. They can also do so with a Google search of teacher rights in the face of those concerns. They can take precautions with students—open doors, desk barriers, camera views, and so forth—so false accusations lack evidence, even potential. Or they can go deeper. In today's society and in part due to the incredible speed of social media, avoiding all such calamities is likely not possible. It is then that the teacher visualizes the worst, at least within the bounds of that particular concern. Disciplinary meetings with their principal, hearings before their school board, and legal entanglements are all things sane teachers would like to avoid. But they can be managed. Contemplating those, reviewing master agreements and complaint policies, will seem daunting at first, but then as they are gradually repeated, they will lead to flow charts, mental or even written—just a series of tasks that have be to be worked through. If one of the worst things occurs—employment termination or even the revocation of the teaching certificate—other jobs, other professions exist. As the teacher negatively visualizes, much of the air of the balloon of crisis can be let out. If the teacher is good at it, it might even suggest the hint of opportunity where only loss was previously perceived.

Negative visualization, though, is not a technique limited to the certificated. One of the ways many noncertificated employees find themselves in trouble is through theft. (To be clear, certified employees of all stripes can find themselves susceptible to this as well.) A clerk who accepts payments skims a few, a custodian who uses his keys to a vending machine to help himself to cash or product, and a purchasing agent who reroutes purchased item to personal use can all wind up in employment and legal trouble as a result. What if they engaged in negative visualization—that is, imagining themselves eventually being caught or even imagining the results after they have already been caught? In the former case—anticipating being fired or frog-walked out of the school in handcuffs—negative visualization would help them correct their path, to stop engaging in these thefts. In the latter case, they could use the technique to begin the climb out of their self-dug hole. Tragic results for an employee can occur when the jig is up if they have never even contemplated that they might get caught. They are trapped by their own lack of self-reflection, their own inability to see any way forward. This technique can help them correct their behavior or, if the ax has already fallen, find that way forward out of the dark forest because they have already considered how to do so many times.

Paraeducators, teaching assistants, may also find this technique useful. One of the realities of the modern classroom, due to special education requirements for the least restrictive environment for students, is the presence of students with emotional and compliance disorders. On occasion such students can exhibit violent behavior, and paraeducators are often assigned to work closely with such students. These paras, though infrequently, become the targets for such violence. They are often provided training in dealing with such students and situations. But this does not change the fact—in fact, in some ways, it reinforces the very real possibility—that they may face a violent or physically abusive young person. This can be a frightening prospect. Educators swap stories of paras and others who are struck or injured and, soon after, end their employment in schools. They didn't sign up for this!

This is an excellent example of people who could benefit from negative visualization. She envisions her usual classroom or smaller room setting where she works closely with a student who struggles with his own physical aggression. They are working on fractions, and the boy becomes frustrated with his inability to master them. She watches as he becomes increasingly agitated. She employs the techniques her special education director has taught her. In her ideation, sometimes they work and sometimes they don't. Perhaps not every day, but on some days, she mentally walks with her student down a scenario in which he finally exhausts his patience and strikes out at her. She thinks through her next steps. She also explores how she feels about being slapped or pinched or struck. As she does, she both practices techniques for preventing the aggression and realizes that she can deal with the unhappy reality of being a target of someone she works every day to help. Aggression that is completely unexpected is certainly more likely to produce trauma or at least distress than that which is expected. And so the fear and trepidation and sorrow accompanying such is drained from it. She achieves a greater sense of tranquility in the anticipation of aggression and also in its actualization.

So what, then, does negative visualization entail? Though the Stoics and, again, some modern psychologists go into the matter at length, creating lists and steps and plans is simply unnecessary. What is necessary is taking some time on a regular basis to engage in it. Marcus Aurelius spent time each and every day, even during military campaigns, on negative visualization. Others found a weekly exercise sufficient. During that time—say just five or fifteen minutes—the practitioner of Stoicism lets loose their fears—small and large, inconveniencing and horrifying—and steps through the process of dealing with them as if they had actually happened. What if I lose my job? What if I could no longer be a teacher? What if I teach too long and suddenly lose my ability to keep discipline? What if I can no longer relate to the latest generation of kids?

Then the visualizer immerses themselves in that reality for just a short period of time. How would I feel? To whom could I turn? How would I deal with the financial loss or the loss of my vocation, my calling? Then he fleshes out the steps to be taken to deal with that crisis. Do it long enough with sufficient frequency, and anything, according to the Stoics, can become manageable. When and if it occurs, the plan will mean that one's tranquility is, if not intact, at least drained of much of its pain.

There is one caveat. Even the greatest Stoics who ever lived have acknowledged this technique would probably not be completely effective in the face of some traumas. In the ancient world of Greece and Rome, the afterlife was understood in a number of different ways, and many of them offered little solace. Bringing people out of abysmal and very much-prolonged grief was a challenge, one addressed in particular by Seneca. As the West increasingly secularizes, a larger swath of the populations today finds itself without the benefit of the promises of a pleasant, even glorious, afterlife. Thus, the Stoic or the person who wishes to engage in this particular technique would probably be wise to start small and to accept that even if you have reached the pinnacles of society—think of Epictetus and Marcus Aurelius—some things may be just too sorrowful to visualize.

There is one objection. Americans tend to be or at least admire positive people. Whole popular philosophies these days talk about visualizing what you want—to imagine your goals as one way to achieve them.

Sometimes, these are just the first step in making actual plans. Other times, though, they are offered as some sort of magic spell, as if just by envisioning something, it will happen. Regardless, these positive visualizations would seem to conflict with the whole negative visualization technique. But really, these are just two roads to joy when done correctly. After all, it is possible to do both. A person could easily take ten minutes every morning—five to envision what they want and five to envision what they do not want; the former, to gain some additional good in life and the latter, to prepare for some evil.

SUMMARY

The Stoic technique of negative visualization is a means by which a person can both prepare for the inescapable reversals of life and drain the misery and despair from them. By imaging on a regular basis those things which might befall them, the Stoic is prepared to deal with them should they befall him and is increasingly inured to the pain they bring. Whether it be job loss, unjust accusation, fear of violence, or any other of the evils that can come in an educator's life, visualizing them in advance can better guarantee that their joy in their profession will remain.

NOTE

1. Seneca, *Moral Essays*, Letter to Marcia, IX.

CHAPTER 4

Stoic Skill 2

Love the One You're With, Appreciate What You Have

Accept the things to which fate binds you, and love the people with whom fates brings you together, but do so with all your heart.
When you arise in the morning, think of what a precious privilege it is to be alive—to breath, to think, to enjoy, to love.
—MARCUS AURELIUS, *MEDITATIONS*[1]

THE END OF CHAPTER 3 LEFT ONE ADDITIONAL OBJECTION ON THE table. That was intentional. It was being saved for this technique. The unstated objection there was that focusing on negative visualization might lead a person to settle, to not accomplish all the wonderful achievements possible in life. One obvious response to this critique is to point to the lives of the great Stoics. Marcus Aurelius was emperor of the Roman Empire, Seneca one of the richest people on earth. Epictetus rose from slave to the pinnacle of intellectual accomplishments in his culture. These were not people whose appreciation for what they had caused them to accomplish or accumulate nothing more.

A second response is taking note of the great pitfall of positive visualization. Call it the Sisyphean response. Sisyphus was the founder and king of what would become the city-state of Corinth. For a while, through cunning, he cheated death both for himself and everyone on earth, until the gods intervened. For this crime against the gods, he was

37

sentenced to spend eternity in Hades pushing a huge boulder up a hill each day only to have it roll back down just as he reaches the summit. The story is, of course, an allegory and a lesson for others whose hubris causes them to strive for too much.

Consider the similarities between the daily struggles of Sisyphus and the busy American. Sisyphus works day in and day out to push that boulder up the hill in order to complete his work. But his work is never complete as, at the last minute, the boulder slips from his muscular grasp and tumbles down the hill once more. The busy American every day puts his own shoulder to the wheel, his nose to the grindstone, in order to find happiness through wealth and the material fruits of his labors. Yet as he accomplishes each new goal—home ownership, a new car, a fine suit of clothing, children enrolled in a private school, a bulging 401K—happiness eludes him, always just slipping from his grasp, attaching itself to some new goal—a larger and more expensive home, a sportier car, more fashionable clothing, a trophy spouse. He reaches his goals, but the happiness he attached to them always slithers through his fiscal fingers.

One modern story exploring this Stoic concept is the "Fisherman and the Businessman," possibly first related by Heinrich Böll. An American business man, it seems, is on vacation on the coast of Mexico when, one day, he watches a fisherman dock his boat and unload his catch for the day. It is still early afternoon, and so the businessman asks the fisherman why he is back so early.

> "I have what I need for today," he responds. The businessman asks about his plans for the remainder of his day.
>
> "I will take my catch to the market and sell it. I will then take the money I have earned home, play with my children, have dinner with my wife, Rosa, and spend some time this evening enjoying music with my friends."
>
> The businessman shakes his head as he hears this. "But why not fish the whole day, until nightfall?"
>
> "What would I do with these extra fish, this extra money that is beyond my needs?" asks the fisherman.

"Why, you would save it and once you had enough, buy another fishing boat and hire others to work for you. As your profits grew, you would busy a whole fleet of fishing boats. With the larger and larger catches, eventually you would control the fishing market, then build a cannery, and provide fish to this whole region, perhaps even to the north to the markets in the United States."

"Is that all?" asks the fisherman, astonished at the grandiose ideas of this visitor to his village.

"No, once you had all this, your payoff would come. Others would marvel at your success and offer to buy out this operation you had built. They would pay you millions. You would be unimaginably wealthy."

"How long would this take?"

"Oh, fifteen or twenty years."

The fisherman reflects on this imagined future for himself. "And what would I then do with such vast wealth?" he asks.

"Why, that is the best part! You would retire and take it easy. All your financial worries would be over. You would spend each day just as you wish—playing with your children, having dinner with you wife, playing music with your friends."

The story speaks for itself. Seneca would have understood its message only too well. "It is not the man who has too little, but the man who craves more, that is poor."[2]

One way of looking at this notion of just being happy with what you have is through the lens of economics, sometimes defined as the science of scarcity. Economic theorists simply assume—and based on the evidence of people in society, the assumption does seem to hold water (oceans of it, in fact)—that scarcity is ubiquitous and eternal. No matter how much a person has, they always want more. Even the wealthiest of economies, operating at full capacity, never reach a point where consumers are sated, that they abandon the shopping malls and their Amazon accounts and simply say, "Enough."

Stoicism, though, directs its follower to do precisely that. As the former slaves offers, "Wealth consists not in having great possession, but in having few wants."[3]

Imagine two brothers, one older and one younger. Both love listening to music with a fondness for classical and a weak spot for the crooners of the 1930s and 1940s. The older brother amasses a large collection of such music, purchasing and repurchasing the selections he likes first on LP, then on eight-track, cassette, and compact disc. As he does so, he saves his money and purchases the players for each technology with the highest fidelity, the sweetest sound. As each improvement hits the marketplace, he sets aside and even discards the older versions, as their pops and clicks, their imperfections, simply cannot stand up to the newer, purer sound the latest brings.

The younger brother can hear the transformations as they emanate from his sibling's bedroom. He, though, has found some radio stations—classical in once case, genuine oldies in another—and listens to his music in this format.

One day, the older brother returns from his part-time job and before hitting the power button on his CD player with floor to ceiling speakers and a rack of components so tall and extensive that not even he is entirely sure the point of each, he hears the music from the radio station coming from next door. He knocks and is greeted warmly by the occupant.

After small talk, he asks, "How can you listen to this? The sound quality is so bad over your radio. The announcers constantly interrupt, and the advertisers pull you away from what is being played with their stupid jingles. You listen to whatever orchestra the DJ happens to be playing when you could listen to only the best. The same goes for the singers on the other station. There is almost always a perfect version of a song, but lots of singers cover it, and you have to listen to whichever version happens to be playing. Why don't you get rid of your radio and go buy yourself a new sound system?"

The little brother has never given it much thought. He has always just listened to his radio. He doesn't want to hurt his big brother's feelings as well. So all he can offer is, "I like my radio. I guess as long as I can enjoy the music from my radio, I just don't see why I'd spend a lot of money to make sure I can't enjoy it anymore."

Most people are like this older brother. Once they find something they like, they look for ways to improve upon it. But they never quite consider that as they seek higher pleasures, they are also ruining simpler ones—the wine connoisseur who wrinkles his nose at any bottle with a price tag under one hundred dollars; the traveler who must leave his own country for a trip to be worthwhile; the eager learner who must attend an Ivy League in lieu of a state school, a community college, or a free book from a library.

The Stoic sees through this. The founder, Zeno of Citium, took this (as philosophers so often do) to a bit of an extreme. He pushed for more and more of less and less. Though his school met with great success and his wealth grew, his lifestyle was well known to include a diet of mostly uncooked food washed down not with wine but water and an almost threadbare garment. He taught in the public forum—beneath the stoa—not in some august edifice built specifically for his school. He taught there in any weather, seemingly inured to rain, cold, and heat. Illnesses, which visited him as they do most people, he took no note of. He viewed the opportunities to improve his diet, his wardrobe, and his physical comfort as largely irrelevant, as posing threats to his long-term happiness. If he could find tranquility in less, why seek more that, proving more difficult to support and thereby unlikely to sustain, would be more likely to disrupt that underlying joy?

Consider how classrooms have changed today. During the baby boom, elementary classrooms often held thirty–thirty-five students. Each student sat in a desk, the seat to which was fastened to a steel bar that ran along the floor, connecting it to the slanted writing space before him. The desk opened to reveal his school texts and school supplies within. Because of the sheer number of students and the mass of their assigned desks, the entire classroom was little more than a sea of student desks lapping against the shore of the classroom walls with a blond, wooden teacher desk, a cloak room to one side, and a long chalkboard spanning the front of the room. There was room for little else. The teacher wrote with dust-less chalk, and the students completed assignments in pencils at their desks. An infrequent treat was a movie threaded manually through the projector, which arrived from some mysterious AV (audio-visual) room.

Today, class sizes have shrunk. Desks and chairs are freestanding. Stations fill the area vacated by the extra desks. The teacher occasionally uses her white board (gone are the days for cleaning chalk erasers out-of-doors), but mostly, she references prepared instructions on her computer, which flash either onto the smartboard from her computer or directly into the student computers through GoogleDocs or some similar software package. Instruction, because it has so many new and varied modalities, appeals to more student learning styles. The costs of such classrooms have skyrocketed, dramatically so from the reduction in student numbers per teacher but also significantly through the constantly evolving technology. (One of the reasons that teacher compensation in America has not increased to the level one would expect based on increased school spending is that so much of it is spent on *adding* staff and teachers rather than enhancing the compensation of an unchanged number of personnel.)

Yet based upon data from the National Assessment of Educational Progress, student achievement in literacy and numeracy is largely unchanged. (To be fair, demographics have changed, and any number of conflating factors may be at play.) Recently, proficiency rates have even declined. So what has been gained through all of this additional spending, the infusion of massive amounts of technology, the attention to learning styles, and the replacement of teachers as the sage on the stage with them as guides on the side?

"Very little," the Stoic would argue. All of the latest bells and whistles have, if anything, led to the unavoidable disruptions that accompany increased complexity. Any teacher who has ever launched into a technology-rich lesson only to find that the technology has failed knows this feeling. The teacher with a box of chalk sitting in his blackboard's tray, facing a classroom full of students seated at their desks with an open notebook in front of them and a no. 2 pencil in their hand, never experienced such technical glitches. If student achievement is basically the same in the technology-rich vs. the technology-poor classroom, why pursue the former? Reports from Silicon Valley hint that technology executives frequently send their children to schools where screens are either scarce or absent altogether.

This is not a Stoic argument for schools and teachers becoming Luddite. Luddites were those nineteenth century workers in England who trashed the latest machinery (power looms, etc.) that was automating much of the textile industry, disrupting their employment in the process. Luddites today are those who reject modern technology for similar reasons or simply because they find the latest innovations to be confusing or even scary.

Rather, this is an argument for conserving tried-and-true teaching pedagogies rather than chasing the educational pendulum with each new arc it makes. Education has a long, tricky history of rushing to every new fad as it arrives at the school's front step. Whole bodies of research have been documented and explored on which teachers are the quickest and slowest to adopt new technologies and innovations. The assumption in all of these analyses is that educators need to be more open to change, more quick to adopt innovations, and less willing to live in the jaded veteran's world view of "this too shall pass."

Yet often, it does precisely that. In the 1980s the IBM corporation produced an instructional program for kindergartners called Writing to Read (WTR). The idea was that teaching students to write would automatically and seamlessly teach them to read as well, thereby, boosting literacy proficiencies at that level. A critical component of the program was the presence of IBM computers in the kindergarten classroom, an unheard-of innovation at the time and also a very expensive one, especially as this was the time before Moore's law had time to more fully play out in classroom technology. The results were stunning. Kindergarten reading proficiency rates in WTR classrooms skyrocketed by the end of the students' first year of schooling.

But then research continued to monitor those students who had experienced WTR. By the end of the first grade, the gap between those who had WTR in kindergarten and those who had not narrowed considerably; it likewise happened at the end of second grade. By the end of third grade, the difference in literacy rates had disappeared entirely. Many researchers concluded that the initial effect was simply due to a more academic kindergarten and the exposure to intense writing instruction as kindergarteners (back when most were still leaning toward the social side). In fact, many educational researchers today have concluded that most early childhood interventions produce immediate results but that they almost invariably fade by the end of third grade. Add all the bells and whistles you want to the kindergarten day, but the results are either artificial—comparisons to classrooms with less academic emphasis—or they are fleeting.

Some countries with high rates of reading proficiencies among their school-aged children, in fact, (Finland and New Zealand, for example) deliberately delay direct reading instruction until age 7, arguing that maturity or brain readiness is more important and leads to more permanent mastery than earlier interventions. Thus, schools that "race to the bottom," intervening earlier and earlier, spending enormous amounts, adding staff, offering professional development, and installing all the latest technologies (as with WTR) may not just experience diminishing returns or impermanent gains but may even be counterproductive.

A related phenomenon can be seen among teachers. A number of years ago, researchers looked at the effectiveness of and parental preference for teachers of various vintages. The extreme cases, for purposes of comparison, were the brand-new teachers straight out of the university school of education program and the gray-haired classroom mavens who were now teaching their first children's grandchildren. Parents flocked to the former. They wanted their children to experience the enthusiasm and excitement the new teachers brought to their students. They wanted them, likewise, to experience all of the exciting new discoveries in the field that these freshly minted college grads would no doubt bring to the classroom.

Learning rates, however, went exactly in the opposite direction. The veteran teacher with a bulging tool box of methods for dealing with discipline problems, student struggles with mastery of content, school phobia, and even student conflicts had multiple approaches to everyday issues and so could seemingly work quickly through all of them on the way to instruction and guided practice. Such teachers are still looking for more and better ideas, but they are much less likely to expend time and effort on that which holds little promise. They are more adept, additionally, at identifying what innovations might actually work and addressing actual problems.

They are better, in other words, at appreciating what they have before them. Rather than constantly seeking out the latest thing, they have reflected upon what works well for them and developed a sense of gratitude for what they have. In one telling illustration of this, Epictetus developed the notion of life as a social gathering with hospitality, as seen with the following example: "Remember that you must behave in life as at a dinner party. Is anything brought around to you? Put out your hand, and take your share with moderation. Does it pass by you? Don't stop it. Is it not yet come? Don't stretch your desire towards it, but wait till it reaches you. Do this with regard to children, to a wife, to public posts, to riches, and you will eventually be a worthy partner of the feasts of the gods. And if you don't even take the things which are set before you but are able even to reject them, then you will not only be a partner at the feasts of the gods but also of their empire."[4]

Some innovations in education do bear fruit. Chalk certainly has its benefits over the stylus; the erasable marker, even more. But the Stoic prefers to await their arrival, once proven, "to wait till it reaches you."[5]

In part, the Stoic approach also respects the law of diminishing returns, the economic rule of thumb that adding more effort and investment into any operation beyond some optimal point will yield less and less benefit per extra unit of such. Computers in classrooms, especially one-to-one programs in which every student has one assigned to him at all times, remain a remarkable innovation, especially to those of the older generations. Yet their entry into the school setting has not been accompanied by any measurable increase in student achievement, other than within the student facility with the computers themselves. Unlike the educational theorists and researchers who always believe some new practice, software, teaching method, or disciplinary model will radically improve schools, the Stoic educator would shy away from such expectations. He would wait until it reaches him. He would wait until the innovation or pedagogical method or technology had proven itself in practice and in the research data before stretching his "desire towards it."

The result is an educator who keeps her focus on tried-and-true practices in the classroom, who is not seeking ever-increasing funding to support new technology expenditures, and who is not exhausting herself in the chase for the educational pendulum. The result is an effective teacher with an underlying tranquility, a deep reservoir of joy undrained by the endless chase.

SUMMARY

While some will argue against the Stoic tendency to give priority to and appreciation for what one has rather than seeking more, modern society is a testament to the result of the Sisyphean pursuit of more of everything in the pursuit of happiness. The Stoic points to the ability to be joyful now with what one already possesses rather than the lifelong delay of such for more. Even the pursuit for refined tastes, as it leaves behind the ability to enjoy what was once greeted with joy, can easily reduce tranquility rather than enhance it. Education, because of its endless focus on the new, the latest, the coming panacea, leaves school people perpetually dissatisfied and, ultimately, exhausted. There may be some advantages to the technology-rich classroom, to software packages that purport individualization and a challenge, and to professional development programs which overturn traditional thinking and offer the latest psychological insights, but even those which meet that promise often do so with a diminishingly small impact, compared to the time, effort, and resources poured into them. Or the impact proves ephemeral, vanishing in the coming years. Meanwhile, the Stoic educator, using his proven tackle, brings in his catch for the day and takes his joy in teaching now rather than at some mythical point in a distant, promised future.

NOTES

1. Marcus Aurelius, *Meditations*, book VI, chapter 39.
2. Seneca, *Letters from a Stoic*, Letter II, On Discursiveness in Reading.
3. Epictetus, *The Discourses*, On True Possessions.
4. Epictetus, *Enchiridion and Fragments*, chapter XV.
5. Epictetus, *Enchiridion and Fragments*, chapter XV.

Stoic Skill 3

Never Fall from Your Purpose

As EXPLORED IN CHAPTER I, THE STOIC PURSUES A LIFE OF UNDERLYING joy by living as human beings were designed to live. Human beings are social creatures, and so that means they need to take care to fulfill the duties owed to others—and not just any duties but, rather, those significant duties: caring for one's children, acting justly towards others, and supporting one's elderly parents. One duty, a truly massive one stretching throughout much of life, is spending that time in a meaningful, important undertaking. The educator may look wistfully at the flourishing businessman, the sports star, and the corporate lawyer, as well as the greater financial success they experience. But in the long run, it is they who will look wistfully at the teacher and the difference they have made, the commitment they honored and kept, to others around them. "If you accomplish something good with hard work, the labor passes quickly, but the good endures; if you do something shameful in pursuit of pleasure, the pleasure passes quickly, but the shame endures."[1]

Shame is probably too strong a word here. Most people don't spend their lives in criminal or ethically dodgy livelihoods, and so they won't necessarily feel shame as they reach the end of their careers or lives. *Breaking Bad*, the story of a frustrated high school chemistry teacher who lets his envy for riches get the better of him, is, thankfully, fictional or at least extremely rare. (Some might argue, nevertheless, that any life's work which does not significantly and meaningfully benefit others is ultimately shameful. Perhaps negative visualization of such a life reflected upon at the end of it would provide the answer.)

If Rufus is correct, the good done by an educator endures and the educator's sense of satisfaction over a life well lived, in that sense, stays with them. Mortimer Adler, the twentieth century's greatest (or at least most well-known) Aristotelian, author of *Aristotle for Everybody*, popularly argued that it was impossible to answer the question, "Are you happy?" until the very end your life. He and Aristotle noted that happiness was not an event or something that comes and goes but, as the Stoic acknowledges, it is something deeper, a reservoir of tranquility largely unaffected by daily trials. Nevertheless, it was possible for a person to live poorly and, in the end, to fail in some fundamental way to live up to one's principles or to live as a human begin ought. Should that happen, such a life was ultimately unhappy.

Thus, the educator's lot in life is one that tends toward joy, but it is not a foregone conclusion. As has become evident during the COVID pandemic and in its wake, many educators—by some estimates, as high as 25 percent—have left the field. Frustration over virtual learning, herculean efforts on their part producing dismal results as students failed to tune in literally and figuratively, the anxieties of pandemic living, a shared perception that things were bad and people hanging onto their mental health by their fingernails, and any number of other factors caused teachers, paraeducators, and principals to find other (what they suspected were) less stressful ways to make a living—greener pastures. As labor shortages worsened, wages skyrocketed and the compensation difference between less challenging employment and education significantly narrowed. This provided some educators with a temptation to leave the profession.

While there were those whose resilience was simply insufficient to endure and others who were probably unsuited to the profession in the first place and were wise to seek other vocations, clearly, some who left should not have. These were true professionals with a gift for teaching and working with young people who are now squandering their talents on lesser endeavors. As they acclimate to the short-term relief of escaping the pressures of the classroom or front office, a small voice in their heads, a Stoic voice, will remind them of what they have lost. They have escaped a rough patch by forfeiting their life's work.

Erik Erikson, the famed developmental psychologist, provides some light on the pitfalls of doing so. Erikson, as will be remembered from those psych courses in the undergraduate school of education requirements, posited eight stages of psychosocial development. In each stage, the human person chose—or had foisted upon them—a personality trait that led to a healthy life or one that led to an unhealthy life. Thus, in the first year and a half of life, the infant comes to develop a sense of trust or mistrust. If parents or other caregivers provide food, love, security, and a nurturing environment, the child learns to trust. If not—think of Harlow's monkey experiments (also in those undergrad psych courses)—the child learns to mistrust. That sense of trust or mistrust, the first stage of Erikson's model, colors the rest of life.

In this chapter's technique—never fall from your purpose—the Stoic is interested in the most distant part of life from trust and mistrust—the very end of life, in fact. This stage brings the choice of integrity vs. despair. It is usually experienced between the age of sixty-five and death. The person achieves integrity when they feel they have accomplished something meaningful in their life, when they have met their sufficiently elevated goals, and when their outcomes have met their appropriate expectations. The person who fails to achieve integrity, instead, faces the final chapter in despair, a bitterness over failures, regrets, and the recognition of a life misspent.

A Stoic would quibble with some of this, weighing such perceptions in a balance that included external forces over which human beings have little or no control, for example, but they would be just that, quibbles. The framework is the same. Integrity, the happiness that sinks deep into the elderly person as she realizes her life has mattered in important ways about positive things, is very much in line with Stoic tranquility.

Covid and its seismic impacts, even its lingering angsts, have dealt so many a bitter hand, inside education and out. Some have virtually collapsed, as can be seen in the astonishing decline in the labor participation rate, church attendance, and the chronic absenteeism rate among students, which has actually doubled since those halcyon pre-COVID days. Even more dire is the nagging suspicion that the worst is yet to come. The possible despair among educators would certainly qualify as that worst. How else could they feel when life's final chapter arrives and they realize that they abandoned the field at the very time students needed them most—that they fell from their purpose and have little or no way to undo what they have done?

That word *fell* is an appropriate one. It reminds one of the man who fell from the top of a skyscraper. Halfway down, a man leans out the window and asks how he is doing. He responds, "So far, so good." Or it is like the man who tells others that he plans to live forever. When queried about the unlikelihood of the goal being met, he has the same response: "So far, so good."

Such a cavalier attitude is possible only when the plummeting man and the improbable immortal ignore the future that is screaming toward them at breakneck (literally in the former) speed. But it is not in the Stoic coda to refuse to face even a very hard reality. It is a violation of the virtue of courage. In some sense, it falls into the vices on either side of the virtue: cowardice in fleeing from reality and foolhardiness in facing that reality without any of the necessary skills and preparation to meet it effectively, head on. Life's end is coming, seemingly accelerating with every year that passes, and joy must be cultivated both now and in anticipation of, in preparation for, that end. When an educator, who understands their life purpose to be the enlightenment of the next generation, falls from it into some field of endeavor of lesser importance, lesser impact, lesser meaning, lesser service to others, they are all but guaranteeing twilight years filled with despair. They leap from the building, mistaking the cool breeze on their face and the freedom that comes with no or lighter responsibilities for genuine happiness, while each passing floor reminds them of the cementitious impact ahead.

So how then do they, instead, hang on? After all, the anxieties that have accompanied the pandemic are real and they are pervasive. Worse, they seem to be setting in. Seneca provides an answer: "In the meantime, cling tooth and nail to the following rule: not to give in to adversity, not to trust in prosperity, and always take full note of fortune's habit of behaving just as she pleases."[2]

How to Hang On

Take those one at a time. Don't give in to adversity. People sometimes make decisions to escape difficult situations that prove to be shortsighted. They imagine that the challenges of the day are never going to end. COVID was particularly problematic in this way because early prognosticators suggested that closing schools and other measures would bring the pandemic to an end within a few weeks or months. This was a false promise, and those in government and health care leadership would have been more helpful if they had at least allowed—publicly—for worst-case scenarios. As the COVID closures and restrictions extended farther and farther beyond the predicted horizon, many lost hope and sought an escape.

Today many are similarly distraught because, though the pandemic is now "over" (or has settled into the background of tolerable human illnesses), certain difficult realities remain: chronic student absences; substitute teacher shortages; a generation of students who learned during virtual schooling that expectations of them have been lowered (early policies during the 2019–2020 school year of awarding grades no lower than the student held when schools had closed and moved to eLearning, regardless of effort or accomplishment, were particularly harmful); more numerous and more severe disciplinary issues; and increasingly demanding parents, unwilling to have their children accept consequences for their behavior. After more than two years of this and with no clear end in sight, it is no wonder that many teachers and other employees are seeking the exit.

The answer to such, though, is precisely what Seneca offered: "To cling tooth and nail to the following rule: [to] not go give in to adversity."[3] The cure, leaving the profession and discovering years later that what has been surrendered is their very purpose in life, is far worse than the illness in part because, even though it is lasting longer than predicted, it is ultimately temporary. Educators, people called to the field, need to stick it out. They need to display courage. There are two exceptions, nonetheless. There are people in the education profession, as in all professions, who do not belong there. Those who discover, as sometimes happens (but less than in the past because of the earlier involvement of education students in actual classrooms *before* student teaching), that they are just not cut out to be a teacher and should find other pastures. But they should do so for that reason and not because of a short-term hiccup in schools.

The second exception is the educator who has truly reached their limit. The problem with this is the lack of objectivity many have about what they can take. The Stoic believes people, especially those who have cultivated it, have vast reserves of resilience. That cultivation is key. Real Stoics do just that, taking and even seeking out life's experiences that boost their resilience. But in the current crisis or postcrisis, it is a bit late for that. As the best time to plant a tree is ten years ago, the best time to add to building stamina is in the past, in terms of the current test. But the second-best time to plant a tree is now, and moving through the current hard times will lead to inner strengths for future challenges. If, however, there truly is nothing left, leaving the field can be the lesser of many evils—that is, emotional breakdowns, self-medicating into addiction, self-harm.

How important is the development of resilience for an educator? Though every role in education faces some controversy and unfair public criticism—how unfortunate it was that the early years of COVID and social media were contemporaneous—a particularly nettlesome one is the school superintendency. If ever an educational job demanded resilience in the face of withering fire, it is this one. Superintendents have many skill sets they must bring to the table to be successful.

One was described in an episode of *Cheers* decades ago. The owner Sam Malone's right-hand man at the bar was an older baseballer nicknamed Coach. Though Sam, a retired pitcher, basked in most of the glory of his past career, occasionally, Coach would find the spotlight shining upon him. Coach, it was said, held the record for most HBPs (hit-by-pitches). He bragged that he could, at will, find a way to wriggle a part of his body into the strike zone and earn a base, the reward for the assumed errant throw by the pitcher. Coach then went on to demonstrate his skill off camera, taking a shot from Sam to the applause of the bar's patrons. In the incredibly competitive environment of professional sports, it is not impossible to imagine an athlete engaging in such, though the speed of baseball pitches would make such both painful and career endangering.

New superintendents often find their initial experiences with grossly unfair, public criticism all but traumatizing. They thought they were ready for it, but they weren't. Such vilification can become especially painful because they are considered, like politicians, public persons. When an individual leaves the role of a private person for that of a public one, it becomes very difficult for them to argue that critiques are libelous or slanderous. Public persons would have to prove untruth; malice; and, arguably, material injury in order to go after their critic. These criteria become such tall orders that superintendents are all but fair game—board members, too, by the way. In an era during which people seem willing to engage in incredible levels of snarkiness, the issue has become much more taxing than usual.

This means, particularly for superintendents, that candidates should gauge their ability to take an HBP. It also means that as milder criticisms come their way, they should use those experiences to develop resilience and personal techniques for acknowledging without internalizing them, except in those cases where they have merit. In part, this means considering the source. More, though, it means considering the validity of the critique. Today, unfortunately, everyone in education has more and faster pitches coming at them, and using such experiences to acclimate to them and build resilience should be a conscious effort.

A second technique for outlasting bad times is to not to trust in prosperity. Prosperity here should be understood fairly broadly. It isn't just material wealth, the good financial times, though that is definitely one important aspect of prosperity. In part, this can be accomplished by negative visualization. The person who spends some time on a regular basis forecasting and facing the negative that may or will come will be better prepared for them.

As with the previous point, this would have been an excellent Stoic practice pre-COVID. It is not unreasonable to believe that those who have struggled most with the aftereffects of COVID in schools were those who never imagined it could get worse, who trusted that the bottom of the pre-pandemic reality would never drop out. One way to *hang on* is to *hold on* to the belief that things will get better. The Stoic would also suggest, though, that another way is to plan for even worse. What if RSV, which saw a marked increase in 2022, continues to worsen and begins striking down attendance levels in early elementary or among the teacher ranks? What if the mask mandates really did create a situation in which student immune systems have been suppressed and influenza rates skyrocket as a result? Educators who consider such ideas—even just the impacts and not the causes—and prepare for them may begin to view themselves as those who can be counted upon in tough times, as people who can step into the breach and serve students even when others drop the ball.

In today's society, an increasing focus on mental health has led people to unabashedly taking care of themselves first, even to the point of taking 'mental health' days off work. The Stoic, except to the extent that the techniques she employs enhance her mental health and toughness, would reject such notions. She would, instead, see the upside of capitalizing on opportunities to demonstrate courage and the other Stoic virtues precisely when the actions of others hint at retreat and surrender. There is resilience and there is courage in this.

The teacher who sacrifices a personal priority in order to report to his classroom because he knows that his absence prevents student learning and adds to the heavy burdens of his peers envisions himself as a person of dedication and courage, as one who does the right thing by others rather than a person who simply cannot take another class session. Having seen the fragile nature of prosperity, he answers the high call of his profession. The principal who, in addition to all of her leadership roles, finds a way to keep schools open when employee attendance is abysmal, who takes a turn serving lunch because sufficient staff cannot be hired when the labor force participation rate has fallen and fifteen-to-twenty-dollar siren calls from the fast food market have depleted applications, can find grim but real satisfaction in meeting the needs of students amid shoestring staffing. The paraeducator who, knowing that parents have dropped the ball for their children because they have surrendered to the problems in their lives and out of their lamentable external focus of control, takes the lead. In all of these cases, their actions are developing, are boosting, their view of themselves as someone who can make a difference, who does not flinch when prosperity gives way to its opposite.

Seneca knew this well when he offered in his work, *On Providence* (2.6), "Unimpaired prosperity cannot withstand a single blow; but he who has struggled constantly with his ills becomes hardened through suffering, and yields no misfortune."[4]

Seneca's final method of not falling from one's purpose is managed in taking "full note of fortune's habit of behaving just as she pleases."[5] This one will be taken up in chapter 13, "Ask Not 'Why Me?' but 'Why Not Me?'"

There is one final point, nevertheless. Seneca said it this way, "The bravest sight in the world is to see a great man struggling against adversity."[6] The assertion here is not that by holding fast during adversity will one's image be enhanced. Rather, it is simply that the person who does step into the breach, who does meet the challenge, becomes a light for others. She emboldens others and lifts them out of their doldrums and self-perceptions as a person who cannot endure, who is weak, and who is not up to the task. In this, the resilient Stoic serves not only her own students well, she creates a positive contagion that means many other students will also be served well.

SUMMARY

Fulfilling one's duties to others is a fundamental obligation of the Stoic because it is a fundamental part of how the human being is designed to live. Not surprisingly, it is also critical to the joy underlying the Stoic's life.

It is of great concern, then, that so many educators have left and seem poised to continue to leave the field in the face of COVID and its aftereffects, both lingering and persistent. For educators to be truly happy, both at present and in life's waning years, they need to stick by their profession, to tap into their resilience when faced with such difficulties. Doing so means not giving in to adversity through courage and developing greater stores of resilience, not trusting in prosperity—ideally in the past—but, even now, as a way of manifesting oneself as a person who serves others even when it is tough and understands that much of life is outside of anyone's control, acting in accord with this perception.

NOTES

1. Musonius Rufus, in Seneca, *Letters from a Stoic*, Fragment 51.
2. Seneca, *Letters from a Stoic*, Letter LXXXII
3. Seneca, *Letters from a Stoic*, Letter LXXXII.
4. Seneca, *Letters from a Stoic*, 2.6.
5. Seneca, *Letters from a Stoic*, Letter LXXXIII.
6. Seneca, *Letters from a Stoic*, 2.6.

CHAPTER 6

Stoic Skill 4

Value That Which Should Be Valued, Despise That Which
Should Be Despised

*At dawn, when you have trouble getting out of bed, tell yourself: "I
have to go to work—as a human being. What do I have to complain
of, if I'm going to do what I was born for—the things I was brought
into the world to do? Or is this what I was created for? To huddle
under the blankets and stay warm?"*
——Marcus Aurelius, *Meditations*[1]

IN THE PREVIOUS CHAPTER, IT WAS ARGUED THAT HUMAN BEINGS CAN-
not be happy unless they are about their life's work, meaningful work
designed to serve others. The true educator who leaves the profession—as
so many have done of late—is all but doomed to a life of unhappiness
and, at its end, despair.

While that chapter spoke of the error of leaving the profession, this
one will speak of the obligations of those who remain within. As must
be clear by now, to ignore these obligations is to lead a life replete of or
reduced in joy.

Think back on the days when newspapers were regularly delivered
by boys walking neighborhoods with large canvas bags slung over their
shoulders or on their bicycles, slinging the latest news over their handle-
bars onto front steps and porches, into bushes and window wells. Though

that rite of passage has not gone entirely away, it is fading quickly, following the milkman toward the exit door. Many boys had moved well into their teenage years before moving onto greater things, while others lasted only a few weeks, their fathers having abandoned their attempts to arouse their progeny in the predawn hours. The child's attraction to a warm bed on a cold morning was simply too much, even in the face of their father's inspiring call to get "up, up, out of bed. There'll be time enough for sleep in the grave."

Yet that is very much the Stoic sentiment toward remaining abed. Not many find their meaning in life through newspapers, at least not on the physical delivery of such (especially these days), but the call to arise from slumber applies to all other works as well. "What was I created for?" asks the emperor Marcus. "To huddle under the blankets and stay warm?"[2]

Without making the comparison, though many Stoics did so, Marcus Aurelius has placed his imperial finger on the difference between the life suitable to a human person and the life suitable for an animal. Pet owners place great store in the companionship and personalities and intelligence of their animals. But if they were to really take an objective look, a data-driven analysis of their furry (or scaly or feathered) friends, they would be forced to admit that a pet's life is spent accomplishing a short list of activities—from most to least time intensive—reproducing; drinking; eating; and, far in the lead, sleeping. Animals, wild and tame, obey their genetic dictates, meet their physical needs, and then minimize expenditures of energy—that is, sleep. Other than these, they have no life's work.

Human beings are made of and for sterner stuff. People have vocations, things to which they are called, and should they abrogate these by measly or by just-less-than-a-full effort, they turn their backs on them. They are the tepid, the lukewarm. They live not as human beings are designed to live. By their own decision making, they abandon, to a lesser or greater extent, their humanity for comforts suitable only for an animal nature. They act as if they were created to stay in their beds, to huddle under their blankets, to stay warm. Whatever else they do, they do only to acquire this comfort.

Consider Epictetus. Raised as a slave and no doubt afflicted by the treatment of slaves, including, by some accounts, the disabling of a leg by the vicious whims of a master, he could hardly be blamed if he found a subsequent life of relative comfort and pleasure attractive, even seductive. That master or, perhaps, a later one sent him to study philosophy in Rome. This education allowed him to open a school of philosophy and become a person of means. Yet he lived in simplicity and owned very little. Long hours of sleep under sheets with large thread counts in a warm bed on a cold morning held no attraction for him. None of that brought joy. None of that *can* bring joy by the Stoic understanding of genuine humanity. Yet Epictetus had great joy, which he found in teaching Stoicism to his many students, in sharing with them the path to a tranquil, joyful, and happy life. It is very much worthy of a human being.

The educator who, through the last few difficult years, has stayed at his post has a real chance at tranquility, both now and much later. But it is only a chance. Some don't grab hold of that chance, that opportunity. The fifty-two-year-old American government teacher who is simply pining for the passing of the final years before he qualifies for his state pension is not better and is, in some ways, much worse (since he hasn't even made room for a teacher of real enthusiasm for his craft) than the one who simply left for a career in insurance or textbook marketing. The third-year seventh-grade science teacher, holding on by the tips of her fingers and lasting only by using up every sick day, every personal day, and every dependent-leave day out of a school calendar (which already has school in session fewer days a year than not), is phoning it in, meeting her (poorly) perceived needs, but she is decidedly not meeting the needs of her students. The fifth-grade classroom teacher who retired three years ago but somehow forgot to tell his principal or the school business office—"quietly quitting," as they call it now—is squandering the precious instructional time purchased by the taxpayers for her twenty or twenty-five students. She is making a mockery of her profession. In all likelihood, she knows it, too, and so what work she does accomplish brings no joy, and the specter of those lost opportunities will likely eventually haunt her into despair.

These should not be confused with the new-teacher-to-veteran-teacher dichotomy found earlier in chapter 4. The difference there was not between youthful enthusiasm and veteran exhaustion but rookie ignorance and old-hand wisdom. That comparison localized just those elements, all else being equal—that is, *ceteris paribus*, as the economists are wont to say. Instead, this is the educator, regardless of years in the profession, who finds no passion in the job, who understands at either the conscious or unconscious level that they are underperforming, holding back a full effort, and diverting their energies and their fervor into something other than their life's work.

This is easy enough to describe, less easy to remedy. So what is the Stoic physician's prescription for such people, those who are regularly putting forth less than a full effort as well as those doing so only now and again?

The initial step is to recognize the problem and face it unflinchingly. In the *Meditations*, Marcus Aurelius says it this way, "The first rule is to keep an untroubled spirit. The second is to look things in the face and know them for what they are."[3] (That something comes before facing a difficult reality is not suggestive of a prior step but simply that an "untroubled spirit" [i.e., a maintenance of tranquility] is the aim of Stoicism and so a reminder that problems are not de facto disruptions of such.) With one step, notice, though, that it has two parts—looking it squarely in the face *and* recognizing it for what it is. The first is a logical necessity. It is impossible to solve an unidentified problem. This is why people have house inspections when buying a home and why home sellers are genuinely surprised to learn they have termites.

For the teacher, one who has told himself he went into the profession to help children or transmit the cultural inheritance of the West to the next generation, this can be easier said than done. Sometimes the easiest person to fool is the one in the mirror. Cognitive dissonance plays a role here as well. When faced with a perception of personal failure (doing a poor job as a teacher) and a belief that education is important, changing the perception of one's performance is a much easier method of resolving dissonance than reigniting enthusiasm for the work, than doing the hard work required of teaching. Thus, the unsuccessful—indolent or apathetic—teacher does not even consciously notice they are so. The Stoic rails against this, of course, arguing that the genuine human person, without falling into discomfort or anxiety, looks objectively at himself and sees that he is not serving students well.

Having done this, he sees it for what it is. That is—owing to the theme that the Stoic is only concerned about things within his control—he sees it as a problem he *owns*. Is student misbehavior a contributing factor to his lack of success in teaching students how to simplify fractions? Are cell phone interruptions, lack of administrative support, computer breakdowns, delayed copier repairs, or dismal parental support part of the problem? Perhaps they are. But whether yes or no, it doesn't matter, as none of that is really within the teacher's control. What is in his control is his expertise, his planning, the animation of his delivery, the development of his relationships with his students. These are the things he can control, and so, having faced the harsh reality of his failure to instill numeracy in his students, he looks there, among these, for it is there—and only there—that they can be resolved. The rest are excuses. The rest are defense mechanisms. The rest are also destructive to his role as a teacher, leading him not to success and joy in education but to an exit or a quiet quit.

There is one aside here. If facing the hard facts sounds familiar, you may have read, as a billion other people seemingly have, Jim Collin's masterpiece *Good to Great*. If that tome can still be found on the bookshelf, turn to the section on James Stockdale and the Hanoi Hilton. Stockdale was clearly a Stoic, and it was, in part, his practice of this philosophy that allowed him to endure the trials and tortures of that North Vietnamese POW detention center, as well as the many fellow countrymen who followed his instruction as the highest-ranking American prisoner there. Stockdale knew exactly what he faced, and he looked it squarely in the eye, drawing on his internal resources—those things he could control—to survive until release was achieved.

The second step must come quickly, for the first one has left the ineffective teacher in a bad spot. He has faced, unflinchingly and resolutely, the problem, as well as the fact that only he can solve it. There is no room here, no space—no defense, no place to hide. The Stoic scorns such protections as unworthy of a human life well lived. It is the career equivalent of standing on the battlefield with no shield and *no cover*.

What is needed, then, is a reacquaintance with the life's work of an educator. This is not about the perks—reasonable salary, state pension, summers (if not off, at least freer and easier)—of such but, rather, the meaning of it. That teaching is worthy of a human being's life is because of its importance to others—students, parents, society, and western civilization—and even its significance to the educator himself for tranquility both now and later.

Some, no doubt, will be too jaded for this. They will be too far gone. The craziness and the obvious opportunities for taking the easy way out so instantly accepted by so many children and their parents, educators, and their supervisors has been too dispiriting. Nothing causes the soldier to lose heart faster and more fully than watching their comrades abandon the field. Retreat is infectious, a contagion. When colleagues assigned student grades based on long-ago performances or at the direction of central offices, the job of holding the line became that much more difficult; in some cases, impossible. As they watched mentors and once-respected teachers head for the doors or lower standards both for others and themselves, bearing the weights of those supports became unwieldly, unmanageable. Almost no external support buttress remained or, in some places, remains to hold high those ideals.

Thus, that support must be found internally. Whatever ideals brought the educator first into the profession can be one source of backing amid an otherwise empty pantry. The Stoic educator must remind herself of what a truly human life is all about: the fundamental obligation to be of service to others and the meaning of the virtues—particularly, courage to reinvigorate her commitment to her profession. And she must remind herself that upon her actions depend her current and future joy, as do her hopes to avoid despair later in life.

Having done so, the Stoic teacher then takes the third, final step, recommitting to education both then and on an ongoing basis. Perhaps at the same time as (or perhaps at a time different than) negative visualization, he can consider what it will mean if the promise of education is increasingly lost in the schools. If students do not master the basic literacy and numeracy skills, if they abandon technical skills taught in career and technical education (CTE) courses in their pursuit of social media, or if they focus so entirely upon extraneous pursuits that underlying mastery of skills is lost, the results can be dire. Economic malaise or even just less growth than would otherwise occur, student inability to compete in post-secondary and market pursuits, a loss of the heritage of Western Civilization, failure in the face of international competition, the decline of public schooling in the face of its competition, and even the sullying or loss of the American form of government are all logical outcomes of a failed educational system. If such big-picture thinking is too artificial for the individual teacher, all of the same can be applied to the students within his classroom. Those results are real, local, and palpable.

As the Stoic practices negative visualization, he can then also engage in a daily practice of reflecting upon the possible outcomes of allowing himself to fail or falter in his duties. Doing so, reminding himself daily of the importance of his craft, will keep it before his eyes, and this is as food to the ravenous animal. It is the sustenance of the human being. Some will argue that a single commitment to this should be enough. But that is like arguing that you only need tell your spouse you love her on your wedding day, that taking a shower once is enough, or that eating is a one and done occurrence. Some things must be renewed, taken in on an ongoing basis. The full understanding of the importance of a life's work is one of those things. The Stoic educator will make the time (as it is one of the few things that is under his control to do) to commit and recommit again and again, especially in the face of the uncontrollable but still disheartening examples surrounding him.

SUMMARY

Chapter 5 spoke of those educators who are considering leaving the profession and how important it is, as human beings, to never fall from one's purpose. Chapter 6 took on the other case, those remaining within but struggling to live up to the high purpose of education, even those who are quietly quitting. Understanding that the profession is currently in tough straits when so many are faltering in the face of so many impediments, the Stoic educator must accept that she can control, fundamentally, only those things over which she has control and her own response to such. That response must mean, first, recognizing the hard reality of the situation and facing it as an individual practitioner with resolve and without reservation. Then, it requires recognizing the inherent importance of education to students, parents, society, and the educator herself and, as a result, the meaningfulness of it as a life's work—as a life's work worthy of a human being. Finally, it requires the teacher, para, and principal to recommit to that life's work, to find the inner strength to not just be a teacher but to do it well.

NOTES

1. Marcus Aurelius, *Meditations*, book V, chapter 1.
2. Marcus Aurelius, *Meditations*, book V, chapter 1.
3. Marcus Aurelius, *Meditations*, book VIII, chapter 5.

Stoic Skill 5

Spend No Time or Effort on Trifles

Because most of what we say and do is not essential. Ask yourself at every moment, "Is this necessary?"

—Marcus Aurelius[1]

By now it must be awfully clear that the Stoic takes life seriously. This is not to say, necessarily, he takes it somberly, with never a grin on his lips or laugh in his throat. Stoics might seem to exude an exaggerated sternness, but this is more about the Roman notion of gravitas than Stoicism proper. Romans, especially political, social, and economic leaders, viewed humor and whimsy as frivolous and as beneath them, outside the behavior expected of them. Thus, they went to great lengths to not be depicted in that way, not even with a smile on their face. This commitment to gravitas remained well into the twentieth century among American political leaders and is why all portraits of American founding fathers are devoid of even the slightest upturned mouth. That many Stoics were Roman and many Greek Stoics were depicted by later Roman artists and sculptors explains how the two are often conflated.

The image of Stoics as serious minded is, nevertheless, an earned one. Simply following the logic that human beings are designed for certain tasks in life, including service to others; that following such innate dictates is the surest path to joy and tranquility; and that deviation from duty will lead to a life without these, even to despair, leads to a conclusion that one's life is not to be taken lightly. All of the Stoics whose lives are outlined in chapter 2 shared this sentiment, and they all, as a result, focused on using time and effort well, to expend it in a manner that will lead to tranquility and joy.

That the zenith of such a commitment is voiced by Marcus Aurelius makes complete sense, for it would be hard to imagine a busier person than a Roman emperor, especially one who is faced with all of the normal business of running an empire as well as defending its borders from attacks by a competing empire to the east and Germanic hordes to the north. If ever a person had no time or effort for trivial matters, it was this philosopher king. But the other Stoics were hardly layabouts. Zeno, Epictetus, and Marcus Rofunius were all running their own schools of philosophy, which might seem like a laid-back job, but the competition was surprisingly fierce. Additionally, Epictetus was forced to spend much time and effort just staying out of the bad graces of those in power. Seneca was one of the richest men in the empire, probably second only to the emperors of his time, and so was busily running his economic concerns while dodging political difficulties. These many concerns no doubt focused their attention on how best to use the finite time they had available to them, but their writing makes it clear that they would have been chronologically attentive even if their schedules naturally demanded less of them.

Thus, the Stoic educator should share in that concern. The emperor makes the point that much of what people spend their time on is nonessential and that they should ask themselves "at every moment" whether or not it is necessary. The point of this is not that life should be free of pleasantries but that time spent on the trivial is lost for the critical. In other words, there is an opportunity cost. *Opportunity cost*, to put it simply, is what a person cannot buy because they buy something else. Buy a Coke and those dollars are lost that could have purchased a Pepsi. Thus, the purchase is less about the loss of a dollar amount than it is about whatever else that dollar amount could have bought. (Fiat currencies, unfortunately, tend to mask that reality.) Spending money on a new car forfeits a home improvement or the interest that money would have earned had it been invested.

But opportunity cost does not apply only to money and economic resources. The essential consideration is that whatever you are expending is a scarce resource, something finite. And what can be more finite than time? Seneca took special note of this in his aptly named work *On the Shortness of Life*: "People are frugal guarding their personal property; but as soon as it comes to squandering time they are most wasteful of the one thing in which it is right to be stingy."[2] And this was not just because Seneca was loaded, though it is often true that the very wealthy do tend to begin allocating their comparably plentiful material wealth to save their much-scarcer time. (Hence, the heiress's hiring or purchase of a private plane, in part, to save the time-consuming process of a commercial flight.) Even had Seneca become destitute, it is clear he would have carefully safeguarded and used his time well, as it is with all of the major Stoics.

Schools are organized and operated on a factory model and an agrarian calendar. Students file into the classroom and spend precisely the number of minutes there as the calendar demands. Should a student or a classroom of students be on the very cusp of a breakthrough at 3:30 p.m., the school bell is unconcerned and unyielding. This is football and when the clock runs out, the clock runs out. It is not baseball, which can theoretically go on forever until that last out is earned. Students who have not learned what they need by day's end go home at the very same time as those who mastered it before morning recess. A third grader (apparently in name only) who is reading at an early, second-grade level does not hold off the start of his summer vacation until his literacy improves. The prodigy and the struggling students have the same number of minutes in the day.

Of all the shortages in education, then, time is the shortest. It is the most finite. Assuming that there is a 180-day school year, a 7-hour school day, and 1½ hours devoted at the elementary level to recess and lunch, teachers are handed 990 hours of instructional time to devote to their students. A secondary school teacher (middle school / junior high and high school) tend to have groups of students for a class period of, to be generous, 50 minutes per day. Thus, the American government teacher, working to edify and inform the next generation of citizens about the theories of governance that infuse the republican form, democratically elected, have 75 hours to do so, 150 if the course is yearlong rather than only a semester. The way the Stoic would view this (and remember, in classical Greece and Rome, liberty, citizenship, justice, and limited government were all notions in far more jeopardy, safeguards more frequently trammeled upon, than in the modern West) is with a furrowed brow and great urgency. Time, as the lawyers say, is of the essence.

The Stoic educator would begin then with careful planning. The curriculum must be prioritized, separating those things which must be comprehended by the students (not just taught by the teacher) from those of lesser or no importance. There isn't time to teach everything society, via state standards, insists must be taught. Careful planning allows for the best and the most important to be sifted out of the dross and the less important. At times this will leave little room for consideration of what a teacher most enjoys. The college literature professor who teaches just one or two authors because he finds them particularly elevating is something of a caricature but one many can point to as very much reflecting an experienced reality. Instead, the teacher must bring to bear their objective understanding of what students most need when they leave in May and, especially, when they descend the commencement stage.

Once the teacher has arrived at this essential curriculum (see E. D. Hirsch's *What Every Xth Grader Needs to Know* for *one* person's sense of such), they then must be ruthless in protecting the important and discarding the trivial. Marcus Aurelius says it this way, "You're better off not giving the small things more time than they deserve."[3] When speaking of matters of Roman governance, this might be comparatively easier to manage than that which must be learned. Schools, as noted in chapter 1, are increasingly called upon to address every social need and every social woe. But every new subject area, every new curriculum, and even every new nuance, comes at the expense of something else. Opportunity cost is alive and well—and treacherous if not recognized consciously and conscientiously—in curriculum when it comes to time allotments. A teacher who fails to plan for such makes the decision to give priority to whatever happens to be taught. The opportunity cost for such a strategy can be incredibly, ruinously expensive.

Once such planning is done and the curriculum harrowed down to that which is of the greatest import, Seneca offers the next step: "Begin at once to live, and count each separate day as a separate life."[4] There is no doubt that to one whose life was fraught with political machinations and existential threats (literally, in the end), this offering had a particular meaning. It is an admonition to take time very seriously, treating it as an incredibly precious resource. He argues that before people—the vast majority of humanity, in fact—really understand the scarcity of time and the need to treat it as such, they inevitably squander it. They treat it as if it were a limitless resource and, thus, something of no value.

Once, however, they can peer into the reality of time, the Stoic understanding of it, they are, in some sense, living for the first time. When people do manage to consider the scope of their entire life, they awaken to the significance of it, at least to them. Viewing especially its end focuses the attention most wonderfully. But most people, for reasons of dread or just a poor attention span, do not or cannot look much in that direction. So Seneca asks them to live each day as if it were a life, packaged with infancy in the morning to geriatric in the evening, and to devote their energies accordingly. In addition to bringing the appropriate urgency to bear, such a strategy also makes life more manageable. The person can now see all of life in a single day, can see that which must ideally be accomplished in this life, how acting in one way or another will end in just the few hours to come.

What would that urgency and that enthusiasm that would accompany the realization of its imminent importance do to a classroom? It would certainly offer a clarion call to many educators—the teacher who eases students into the first day of school in the fall, touching on the syllabus or the birthday wall and offering no actual instruction on what must be learned. The principal who holds a school assembly on all sorts of pretexts with little or no regard to any nexus between the content of such with what students must learn. The parent organizations, clubs, and activities who use instructional time for fundraisers (the money simply representing the value, in some sense, of instructional time), oblivious to the fact that taxpayer expense for that time easily outweighs any fund-raiser gains. The para who takes a mental health day (a term predating COVID but whose popularity has ballooned during it).

Were such educators to gain a better understanding of the essence of time and the Stoic understanding of it, how quickly things would change. Having carefully planned a curriculum around the most vital learning students must master, the starting pistol rings out, and the race is on. Would a competitive runner pause to admire a flower growing by the side of the road? How much more important, to poorly paraphrase St. Paul, is what students must know as a result of their schooling than a laurel wreath which will wither and fade?[5]

The problem, even for those who have once realized the critical importance of time in education, is maintaining the focus and the effort. Like dieting, it is easy to begin with a plan, tougher to hold to it when Christmas goodies appear and birthday cakes light up. A school year, though briefer (and therein lies part of the problem) than work years in most endeavors, can still be a bit of a slog, especially when students misbehave, parents complain about too much homework, and colleagues take on a more leisurely, less enthusiastic pace.

That is where Seneca's image kicks in. "Count each separate day as a separate life."[6] That consummate wit George Bernard Shaw supposedly said, "Youth is wasted on the young." What he meant by that, given his sardonic nature, is not entirely germane here, but it is nevertheless a discouraging reality that youthful enthusiasm is often accompanied by lack of skill, while the deep competence of the aged, earned through experience, is so often devoid of energy. If only the two could somehow be combined. Seneca offers a mental technique for doing just that. The elementary teacher, master plan in hand, engages it with the vigor of the morning (youth if the day is a life) and with the competence of the plan itself and her own experience intact. The best, most important things are attacked first and those of lesser importance (though she should never reach the unimportant, given the scope of today's curricula and societal expectations), later in the day as energies flag, into the day's old age.

The secondary teacher who is unable to teach in such a way (since his periods are assigned by others) can accomplish the same within each class period, should treat each "as a separate life." He begins instantly upon the bell's final peal (or, among some of the greatest instructors, before the bell, as nothing brings students so punctually to class as a teacher who drives forward with eager determination, making it crystal clear that what he has to offer is important, too important to wait for such silly realities as class start times). He, too, leaves the less important for the end of the day, but he doesn't fritter away this time (as does the true squanderer whose students gather at the classroom door three minutes before the end of the period so they can be the first in the hallway when the chimes sound) either. He uses it for closure, student-led summaries of what has been learned, reinforcing the accomplishments of the day. He teaches, as they say, to the bell or a bit after it. Why not?

Even with all this, though, Seneca means a bit more. It is not just that the day should be treated analogously to the life, it is also that the day should be treated with the reverence extended toward a life. When people, even the not terribly reflective, stop to consider their entire life—what is over, what is now, and what may be to come—they tend to become quiet. They revisit regrets (not, to be clear, a Stoic thing to do), examine their satisfaction with their current lot in life, and at least ponder next steps. When people, however, stop to consider their day (if they ever do), they don't treat it with anything like the same regard. Yet a day is simply one discrete portion of a life. One might argue that the whole is more than the sum of its parts, but it is hard to imagine a series of dissipated parts adding up to a well-lived whole.

Thus, each day gathers a sense of urgency, of newly understood importance. Every school day not utilized to its fullest is a wasted—or at leased materially reduced in value—day, one that can never be gotten back. Something important—since the teacher has carefully selected and crafted her curriculum plan to include only that which is important or most important—will be lost if she phones it in. The lessons are taught deliberately, aimed at those areas of learning that are most critical for her students to learn, day in and day out. If such a course of instructional action is pursued, it is hard to see how these deliberate days will lead to anything but a deliberate week; year; and, ultimately, life, for each day is a life.

The alternative, Seneca has written to his friend Lucilius is to play the fool who "is always getting ready to live."[7] Days are seductive because they are short. One can always make recourse to turning things around later, to become a great teacher later, to prioritize instruction next week, once Homecoming week is over or Christmas is behind. But with every day frittered away, so is a life.

The Stoic educator will then first prioritize a curriculum plan, giving priority to that with most importance. Then he will spend every school day as if it is a whole life, fully engaging students and taking advantage of the cycles of a day to exploit those times when students are most ready to learn but leaving no time unused in productive pursuits. Finally, he will bring to bear those instructional techniques most suited to the lessons to be learned. This requires attention to detail, careful analysis, and genuine care.

Marcus Aurelius offered his sense of how to approach such. "Concentrate every minute like a Roman—like a man—on doing what's in front of you with precise and genuine seriousness, tenderly, willingly, with justice. And on freeing yourself from other distractions. Yes, you can."[8]

That *man* part shouldn't be off-putting. He means *human*, and to the extent he means man, he was simply using that as a way to call himself and others out, a private statement with public intent to rise to the occasion and dig deep. In the classroom this means several things. It means focusing not on what has been taught but what has been learned. The Stoic teacher has gone to great lengths to lay out her instructional plan so that which is most important is given priority. How utterly meaningless, then, to teach it without regard to what has been learned. Getting to some lesser content, covering all the material, cannot be given precedence over what has been taught but has not yet been learned. This requires the committed teacher to engage in some type of formative assessment in which what has been learned or what has not been learned affects the instructional plan going forward.

It also means *engaging* the students rather than just presenting to them. The reason Ben Stein's performance in *Fast Times at Ridgemont High* ("Anyone, anyone?") is so funny and painful at the same time is that everyone has sat in such a classroom. Watching a teacher with the necessary knowledge but no sense of its success or failure in reaching students is excruciating. And that was in the age before cell phones, those addictive little techno-demons that are swallowing up student attention and pulling them away from classroom lessons. Forty years ago, teachers and principals lamented the entertainment value of Big Bird because he set such a high standard for delivery of learning. The intentionally minuscule durations of *Sesame Street* skits didn't help either. Solid educators, though, responded with increasingly engaging instruction on their part. Now teachers would love to go back to the Big Bird days. Big Bird didn't bring friends to you twenty-four seven or alert you to the latest posts on social media or report in with the latest cat or insane and borderline-erotic videos.

It would be preferable to revert to those earlier days before young minds were being retrained for astonishingly short attentions spans and unreplicable entertainment values. But the Stoic wastes no time wishing that things were other than what they are. Instead, he plots a strategy for solving the problem in the arena that he can control—that is, his classroom. This may mean a combined strategy of excluding cell phones at least within the classroom, or even just visibly so, but it must also include a commitment to finding ways to become more engaging, to not allow students to do their own quiet quitting, to infuse lessons with purpose statements that do appeal, and to find new learning activities that students will tune into. This is second nature to the elementary teacher, less so for the secondary, particularly the high school teacher who considers himself to be a content specialist first and a teacher second. (How much worse is it at the postsecondary level!) Thus, the Stoic teacher recognizes the need to develop skills of engagement and that pursuing the Stoic commitment may very well entail becoming much less stoic.

Summary
Stoicism's commitment to a serious approach to life causes it, ineluctably, to focus on the importance of time. This is a scary proposition for the educator pursuing a Stoic ethic because there is so much to teach and so little time in which to teach it. The solution, given that finding one within personal control is the only logical approach, is to be sought in

the classroom. Thus, the teacher gathers together state standards and curriculum guides and school instructional policies and carefully crafts a prioritized set of learning objectives for her students to master. This involves a merciless culling of the trivial and even just the less important. It also means taking the instructional day extremely seriously, a separate day as a separate life, carefully considering the cycles of the day as students experience them and utilizing each and every minute as a precious opportunity never to be squandered. It also means bringing the teacher's best game to the classroom, considering what must be learned and whether it has been learned over what must be taught, and stepping up to the new realities of student engagement in a world that has beat a path to the pupil's door and raced to the bottom of attention spans and popular—sometimes sordid, always distracting—content. Becoming a Stoic teacher is a tall order. Who said it wouldn't be?

NOTES

1. Marcus Aurelius, *Meditations*, book IV, chapter 25.
2. Seneca, *On the Shortness of Life*, XLIX.
3. Marcus Aurelius, *Mediations*, book IV, chapter 32.
4. Seneca, *On the Futility of Planning Ahead*, CI.
5. 1st Corinthians, 9:25.
6. Seneca, *Letters from a Stoic*, On the Futility of Planning Head, CI.
7. Seneca, *Letters from a Stoic*, On the Futility of Planning Ahead, CI.
8. Marcus Aurelius, *Meditations*, book II, chapter 5.

CHAPTER 8

Stoic Skill 6

Death and Focusing on the Controllable, Ignoring the Uncontrollable

MOST PEOPLE WHO WORK IN SCHOOLS HAVE A SOFT SPOT IN THEIR hearts for the school library. More than twenty years ago, there was a concerted effort made by librarians (a.k.a., media specialists) to change the name of these delightful refuges from the vicissitudes of the world and repositories of wisdom and delight to "media centers." It was an unfortunate attempt to erase a highly evocative word and replace it with a technocratic, wonky phrase. The effort gained a lot of steam in its earliest years but, thankfully, today seems to be losing much of it, as the advent of e-Books has seemed to coincide with the return of the earlier name, library, to these still book-lined rooms.

Early in the last century, just in case children in elementary school libraries struggled to find a book—a rare event, in fact—or a teacher required information on which books to recommend, two medals came along that helped, the Caldecott for the younger set and the Newbery for those a bit older. Awarded by divisions of the American Library Association, the medals were intended to recognize distinguished children's literature and serve as a guide for children and those serving them in schools. The Newbery came first, starting in 1922, and the Caldecott, a bit later, in 1938. It is interesting to read through the winners for each year and to take note of which have stood the test of time and which have been largely forgotten.

One unfortunate example of the latter is the very first Newbery Medal winner, *The Story of Mankind*. Written by Hendrik Willem van Loon, a Dutch American and an exceptionally popular author, this honored tome does just that: it tells the story of the rise of homo sapiens from the very beginning to the start of the twentieth century. In its opening he attempts to describe to children just when is meant by eternity: "High in the North in a land called Svithjod there is a mountain. It is a hundred miles long and a hundred miles high and once every thousand years a little bird comes to this mountain to sharpen its beak. When the mountain has thus been worn away a single day of eternity will have passed."[1]

For such a spirited attempt to get across to children an ethereal notion like eternity, van Loon surely earned his medal.

Whether Epictetus or Seneca would have appreciated the imagery or the work to transmit the long view to children is uncertain. But they would certainly have agreed with the importance of taking that view. Specifically, though, the Stoics did not see advantage in contemplating eternity but, rather, the contemplation of death. Marcus Aurelius made the distinction well: "Brief is man's life and small the nook of the Earth where he lives; brief, too, is the longest posthumous fame, buoyed only by a succession of poor human beings who will very soon die and who know little of themselves, much less of someone who died long ago."[2]

That the emperor should discount the ability of someone to enjoy posthumous fame is ironic but still basically correct. Though few will be remembered as long as Marcus Aurelius, it remains true that even he will eventually be forgotten. At some point in the distant future, his name will fall out of the books, or the books themselves will fall. And even if he and they don't, notice that he hints at yet another reality about posthumous fame. Even if people in the future do remember someone, what they know of him will be much less than the little they know of themselves. What does anyone really *know* about Marcus Aurelius and, additionally, how is that vanishingly small fame of even a great person a benefit to that person?

What consideration of death offers is something else. To continue with the imperial wisdom, "Don't behave as if you are destined to live forever. What's fated hangs over you. As long as you live and while you can, become good now."[3] In other words, without acknowledging in a genuine way that they will die, it becomes easy for people to decide there is plenty of time to improve themselves or attend to a task *later*. Understanding that life is finite, that there will be a time when time itself runs out, can dissuade them of that. In his work *The Life of Boswell*, Samuel Johnson offers the following notion in a pithy way: "Depend upon it, Sir, when a man knows he is to be hanged in a fortnight, it concentrates his mind wonderfully."[4] Well, as it turns out, *everyone* is going to be hanged in a fortnight. The "hanging" may occur in different ways—cancer, old age, falling down and breaking a toe, or committing suicide by order of the emperor—and the fortnight might be longer (or shorter) than fourteen days, but the noose still pulls just as tight. Thus, contemplating death can be a useful tool for motivating people to better use this day and all the days ahead. *Carpe diem*, as the motivational speakers still say.

But why should contemplating death even be necessary to convince people to bring their ships into the wind, to get about the important tasks of life and living? There are at least two answers. One is simply to shake one's head and accept that this is just part of the human condition. People prefer not to think of their own demise, and this reality is simply to be accepted. That it threatens the good life is out of people's control. It can be addressed but not removed. This would be the traditional Stoic response—people are afraid of death and so they will, without their own intervention, avoid thinking about it and that is just how things are (which is not to say that they can do nothing about it but more on that soon).

A second response was offered by researchers at Bar Ilan University in Israel. In 2019, they published the results of a study that argued that ignoring one's personal death, as opposed to the death of others, is a biological reality, one that is brain- (i.e., neuron-) based. This is to say that people understand that everyone is going to die but that people also believe they are the exception. Extrapolating from and beyond that research, it is possible to posit but not prove why that might be. Evolutionarily, focusing on death would cause apathy or despair, which would then lead to a reduced focus on reproduction and child rearing, violating the Darwinian mandate. Thus, those who spend time considering their own personal demise naturally select themselves out of or reduce their impact on the gene pool. Those who fail to deny the existential threat become victim to it. This is possible, but it's hard to prove.

The point of all this is that human beings naturally recoil at the idea of their personal death and so spend no or very little time considering it. This is disastrous, from the viewpoint of the Stoic. The result is that people, unless they intervene to alter the perception, go blissfully through all or the vast majority of their lives with no sense of urgency about becoming virtuous, about accomplishing the tasks appropriate to a human being, about doing and believing that which will bring them deep, abiding joy. As Marcus Aurelius has put it, "It is not death that a man should fear, but rather he should fear never beginning to live."[5] The person—which includes most people—who fails to acknowledge the coming reality, who cannot face that reality with undaunted stare, will never truly or fully live.

This staring into the maw of the reaper is the means of finding the urgency of living well. Stoics then and still today, as well as many religious denominations, pursue this through the process of memento mori, a concept already explored in chapter 3. This is consistent with another major theme of the Stoics—attention given to only those aspects of life which are under one's personal control. The ancients drew a fairly black-and-white distinction between those aspects of life under the individual's control and those not under his control. Modern stoics tend to view control on a continuum, with some things highly controllable (what they'll eat for breakfast), some not at all controllable (a meteor strike), and most things somewhere in the middle (your child's health). Thus, to turn things back upon themselves, the ancients viewed death as outside of one's control but the *perception* or *interpretation* of death as within their control. Thus, the Stoic stares down death but interprets it not as a disaster but as a tool to be used to maximize life, to spur the person on to live in such a way that it adheres to the Stoic virtues and serves in the pursuit of tranquility.

But the call to ignore that which is out of one's control, *everything* that is out of one's control no matter how concerning, and attend entirely to those in one's control extends far beyond the notion of death.

"Some things are in our control and other not. Things in our control are opinion, pursuit, desire, aversion, and, in a word, whatever are our own actions. Things not in our control are body, property, reputation, command, and in one word, whatever are not our own actions."[6]

What, then, is the import of these lessons on death and control for the educator seeking greater joy from her craft?

One of the effects, still lingering in the aftereffects of the COVID pandemic, was a tendency, even a need, to hunker down. With so many schools across the country surviving (barely) on eLearning and all of its really inadequate offerings, the bar was set lower. Even in schools in which students and staff were physically present, there was still a sense that things were different. The message was spread quite liberally that just showing up was a victory. When students and their teachers did show up, they were still surrounded by all manners of strangeness—masks, barriers, barrels of sanitizer, obstacles to proximity, and even the notion of staying home with the sniffles as heroic (which led to chronic absenteeism)— that made school less like regular school and more like the half day to allow staff to attend afternoon professional development or those rump hours after lunch and before the 2:00 p.m. Halloween party. Times were stressful, and those working in schools, like pretty much every professional eventually, were declared heroes for just showing up.

For many—for most—this made it difficult to move on to better things, to innovate, to set higher student achievement goals because they were either struggling or were trying hard to be considerate of the many others who were. It was enough to just make it in and keep the lid on. This (again, for many) became a habit. A new norm was achieved. What would once have been deemed a shameless phoning it in was enough. Going beyond that was not expected and even discouraged. A wonderful cinematic example of this can be found in the vastly underappreciated 1988 film *The Adventures of Baron Munchausen*. In one scene, during the siege of Vienna by Turkish armies, a soldier is brought before the city administrator, a "man of reason," i.e., of the enlightenment, for having accomplished incredible acts of bravery. Rather than awarding him a medal or recognizing him in some other way, the administrator orders his execution because his extraordinary actions are demoralizing to his comrades, who are trying to go about their (war) business in simple, ordinary ways. In an instant bravery was redefined as deviant or gauche. During the pandemic a similar thing happened in schools. Pushing too hard, asking too much, and showing up even when not feeling the best in order to serve the kids was discouraged and, in some cases, even vilified.

That pandemic reality has unfortunately become a trend and, again, for many, a habit. Habits are such hard things to break. Breaking them means taking assertive or, if the habit is addictive enough, extreme measures. The Stoics offer the steadfast contemplation of one's personal death as such a measure. Understanding that there may very well not be time to get better or do more or become the ideal teacher later should concentrate the mind on the need to do it now, today. Since this is a professional pursuit rather than a personal one—the ancient Stoics often cautioned their disciples to envisage death so that they would start today to become a better person, to cleave to greater virtues in life, rather than procrastinate and ultimately ignore it. (Plus, in the ancient world, as opposed to today, the specter of unexpected or sudden death was far more real, more likely, and seemingly always crouching nearby.) Still, since the educational profession is a worthy way to spend one's life, waiting to get better at it should be discouraged by the recognition of personal death since it is still waiting for everyone.

Another approach, though, would be to deal with professional procrastination by a recognition of professional death. Even should a teacher live to be one hundred, it is unlikely they will work beyond the age of sixty-five, and many will retire as early as fifty-five. Since teachers typically begin their careers at around twenty-two or just a year or so later, even a full career is rarely more than thirty-five years. A new teacher may look at thirty-five years as a very long time. A veteran knows better and watches, wistfully, as the annual cycle of the school year—and schools most definitely have their annual rhythm—spins more quickly over time.

Thus, perhaps the reality of retirement can concentrate the educator's professional mind. Retirement should not be a focus (as it is unfortunately for some), as some yearned-for, sweet release from an unhappy career but, rather, like death, as a clarion call to greater efforts. The principal who waits to get better—to enact a new, promising program in their schools, to really get after students with chronic absenteeism, to bring in eSports so that an underserved student population can find a meaningful connection to their schools as those in more traditional activities do—is very much in danger of never becoming the principal she imagines she will become. Or those problems she will address in two or three years will go unaddressed and those students, unhelped, in the meantime. Retirement as professional death could be one way to focus a less than fully invigorated educator to better and more immediately challenge herself once again.

So what, then, of this matter of control? This was discussed briefly in chapter 1 as a matter of wisdom, as the Stoic understands it—that is, knowing the difference between good and evil and clearly recognizing the difference between things they can control and things they cannot control. The moderns also include the notion of things that are partially within one's control, a very large group (and an important one to note), though it does muddy the clearer waters of the ancients. If control really does exist on a continuum, then the Stoic educator is better off pursuing ends that are either completely in his control or at least very much closer to that end of that range.

Consider the unexpected assembly. Assume the situation of a truly dedicated Stoic educator teaching sixth-grade world history. She has carefully planned her school year, focusing on those cultures and events which have the greatest bearing on the lives her eleven- and twelve-year-olds will experience in a changing world. She has identified the salient features of each, picking and choosing what an educated person should or needs to know in the future. As a committed history student in college, she endured much pain in this process because time limits (on school periods and the school year) meant she could not spend all of the time she so desperately wished to on so many truly engaging historical eras. She wanted to put before her students the entire feast that is world history, but the academic year would only allow so much. Anything that made it in meant, ultimately, that something else was left out (another example of opportunity cost).

After a seemingly endless struggle and literal psychic pain, she finally arrived at a manageable curriculum with the highest priorities included to be offered to her students. Then on Thursday of Homecoming week, the principal announces a pep assembly for the next day. It will gobble up most of first period. Suddenly, something else must be dropped. Not only that, but because she teaches the same subject matter (a prep) three times over the block schedule that they use, her periods two and four classes will have sufficient time for their lesson, but period one students will not. Her carefully crafted lesson on Athens, the importance of Socrates, Plato, and Aristotle, the meaning of Hellenistic architecture, and the relevance of Greek political theory is now in ruins—or it can still be pursued, but it will mean deleting some later topic during the school year, something she must specifically identify if she is not to experience the laissez-faire catastrophe of just dropping whatever came at the end of the year, a disaster because more modern topics tend to be more relevant than less modern.

Regardless, she is furious. So she sets up a meeting with her principal to discuss the matter, explaining her hard work and preparation and the realities of teaching history when school calendars make opportunity costs so incredibly expensive. But he clearly enjoys futzing with the school calendar and schedules. He sees Homecoming events and other occasions, including even those that are less able to be anticipated ahead of time, as part of the school culture, part of what remains of fun in schools. He wants to be supportive of her but just doesn't see the big deal of dropping in a few pep assemblies and other ad hoc events (though he wisely doesn't use the phrase "big deal" in their meeting). After all, he notes, they do miss some days or start school late or early for weather events. She explains that she does understand that and, in fact, figures in three days for such each year when she's prioritizing her teaching and plans her instructional schedule. "Good for you," he almost replies but, tactfully, doesn't.

So now what? Now the teacher needs to decide if this is a courage issue or a wisdom issue. In pursuit of courage, she has fought the good fight, but does that virtue now demand that she continue the pleas or, in acknowledgment of the Stoic principle of ignoring that which cannot be controlled, drop the matter and go back to the sad task of eliminating perhaps one or two more periods in her already bare-bones curriculum? In this case, though the details of the actual situation would certainly matter (the probability he will change his mind, possibility of vindictiveness, etc.), she has probably now done what she can and will simply have to write this off as something uncontrollable. Given that she is a Stoic educator, she drops the matter with her administrator and instigates a solution, even though it is a less satisfying one, herself. After all, the Stoic always asks first what she can do to address situations, understanding that receiving solutions from others is always much, much less likely.

The application of the controllable/uncontrollable technique is wide and long. The effective, engaged teacher teaches instantaneously with the bell or even before it and continues until the ending bell, even explaining to his students that "the bell does not dismiss class. I do." But the school office insists on leading the flag pledge each day through the intercom and frequently, because of all the busyness of that sometimes-besieged entry point, doesn't get it started until thirty seconds or a full minute or two after the bell. Lost is that amount of time, significant when aggregated over the space of a year, as well as the sweet spot for instruction, the very start of class. Is this a case of something that can be controlled—can the classroom PA be muted, perhaps—or not?

Is Wednesday night set aside for no homework, even though this often fits poorly with the best assignments for the lesson that falls on the next day? Are students removed from classrooms by the guidance counselor at really difficult times? Are school athletics pulling students out of the classroom at rates far beyond the limits for what will negatively impact learning? Are dress-up days both disruptive and increasing in frequency? Are teaching methods, as in reading or writing instruction, set at the district level rather than providing for the teacher's autonomy? All of these, to the classroom instructor working hard to maximize learning, can be sources of concern. If these practices are required, does that make them uncontrollable, or could they be controlled if the right teacher advocate serves on the right committee?

The key for the Stoic educator is to assess the situation. If it is controllable, he should apply his best efforts to making a positive difference.

If it is not controllable, though, he should drop the matter as a waste of time. After all, a teacher's time and energy are finite, and expending them on things beyond his control also has an opportunity cost. Better to spend those valuable resources on something that can be controlled, that can be improved upon. Additionally, if it is not controllable, he should drop it entirely, not make it a source of regret and unhappiness. That is truly one of the most important aspects of the Stoic approach. That which cannot be controlled should be dropped, should be dismissed as unworthy of any effort or mental duress. Continuing to engage with the uncontrollable is a waste—a waste of time, effort, and mental focus.

SUMMARY

For the Stoic, death is an interesting point of discussion, as in, it is mainly out of one's control, it is not worthy of much consideration. However, as a means of focusing the mind, attending to those things in life that are worthy and doing so *now* rather than waiting until it is too late, death is very much something upon which to reflect (i.e., memento mori). That such techniques are necessary is the result of an apparently brain-based tendency for human beings to deny or ignore the inevitability of their own death. Thus, that a person will die is out of their control, but their reaction and interpretation and productive use of that fact is very much under their own governance.

And what is and is not controllable is important in all aspects of life, not just its demise. The Stoic educator will use the virtue of wisdom to determine the difference. When he determines that it is outside of his control, he will not only fail to initiate or continue efforts for change, but he will eradicate it from his mind. He will waste no mental energy, no regrets, and no lingering anger or unhappiness with it. For if he did, it would be an unnecessary and unproductive disruption of his tranquility and his joy.

NOTES

1. Van Loon, , *The Story of Mankind*, p. 1.

2. Marcus Aurelius, *Meditations*, book III, chapter 10.
3. Marcus Aurelius, *Meditations*, book IV, chapter 17.
4. Johnson, *The Life of Boswell*, p. 171.
5. Marcus Aurelius, *Meditations*, book XII, chapter 1.
6. Epictetus, *The Enchiridion*, book 1, chapter 1.

CHAPTER 9

Stoic Skill 7

What the Well-Dressed Stoic Is Wearing These Days

FIRST OFF, DRESSING LIKE A STOIC DOES NOT MEAN WEARING A TOGA, even if the ancients would have certainly done so. Neither does it mean purchasing a whole new wardrobe. Possibly, how one dresses isn't a skill at all. But Stoic principles do imply certain attire selections. As a matter of fact, it is even possible to shop at a store specifically created to meet the demand for Stoic clothing. It is called Stoic Store UK, and the main page of its website features the most recognizable image of Marcus Aurelius. While the emperor cannot object, one suspects he would not appreciate being used as a marketing tool. Then again, he would probably recognize the matter to be out of his control—given that he has been dead for more than eighteen centuries—and so accept it with no further, wasted consideration.

One way of determining how a Stoic would dress is to look at the ancients, adjusting for the fact that attire was very different when compared to today. (Outside of frat parties, togas are astonishingly scarce.) Zeno of Citium, a Stoic founder, as part of his overall ascetic lifestyle, was often seen in well-worn garments, sometimes described as threadbare or even tattered. Thus, the very first proponent of the Stoic school set the stage. Surely, Epictetus, when a slave, also wore the clothes of such—that is, rough, sturdy, and inexpensive. That probably changed when he left for Rome to study philosophy, but this is largely conjecture. Would Seneca have dressed like a beggar? It is doubtful. As an incredibly wealthy man,

Seneca would certainly have been demanded by Roman society to dress the part, at least when out in public, which would have been most of the time for one with expansive interests both mercantile and political. As for Marcus Aurelius, as emperor, he certainly could not have attired himself as a slave or simple workman. Like all political leaders, he wore the uniform of his post. When leading military expeditions, he did likewise.

Of the few teachings specifically on this topic by the Stoics, perhaps the most revealing is from the *Discourses* of Epictetus, in a section called "On Finery in Dress." It opens with a learned young man approaching the philosopher. He is noted as having "hair dressed more carefully than was usual and his attire in ornamental style." This immediately sends Epictetus into a discussion about what makes dogs, horses, and other animals beautiful. He concludes, and the younger man has no disagreement, that what makes them beautiful is their consistency with their best nature. Thus, a beautiful dog is one who is loyal and useful. A beautiful horse is one which obeys its rider and goes about its task, whether farming or battle, with obedience and diligence. A beautiful person is also consistent with his nature, the nature of a human being, and, thus, one who demonstrates wisdom, restraint, courage, and justice.[1] Notice that none of this has anything to do with bodily adornment. Can it, then, be ignored?

It probably cannot. Why, without even being asked by the younger man, does Epictetus launch into a discussion of beauty? He does so because he recognizes in him an error, an unstated but very clear tendency of his to equate beauty with carefully coiffed hair and fancy dress. Remembering that Epictetus's works were not actually written by him but memorialized by his students later (which places him in good company with Socrates, Jesus Christ, etc.), it still seem clear that the philosopher was railing against such unnecessary adornment as a distraction from where beauty truly lies: in pursuit of virtue. But then, in what must seem a familiar conundrum to the moderns, Epictetus is torn about how to truly raise the issue. If he says nothing, he leaves the young man in error. If he does make a frank comment, "Set my hair straight . . . stripped off my decorations . . . stopped me from plucking the hair out of my body," he fears it will insult the potential student and drive him away from the great truth that can be found there.[2]

It is the very same condition of the modern parent when their child comes home from college dressed scandalously or behaving in some unacceptable matter. Do they say nothing and so silently endorse it? Or do they lay out their concerns and potentially drive their child away? Epictetus does not dance around the issue so much as he elevates it to a higher realm of discourse, hoping that doing so will make the point without piercing him with it. He quite literally verbalizes the horns of his dilemma, the perils of both silence in the face of this dandy's adornments and speaking, which may create an affront and, thereby, break all ties. The young man's response to this specific issue is unrecorded.

Though on less solid ground than many of other Stoic principles and techniques, there is still enough here to inform the Stoic educator.

As educators fulfill their responsibilities for the benefit of students, it might be best to begin there—specifically, with dress codes. Such school policies once had at least a dual function. They were designed to coop-erate with parents, providing a united front of what constituted appro-priate attire for young people in a public setting. While a small minority of parents occasionally raised objections, concerned that their children's free-expression rights were being trampled, most appreciated the backup. Free to argue that short skirts or long hair were inappropriate in and of themselves, they were also free to fall back upon the fact that the school would not tolerate them in any case. The result was a shared social contract between the parents and those *loco in parentis*, those legally rec-ognized as being able to act in the stead of parents at school, where the actual parents were not present. Though the flash points—where students rebelled and parents backed them up—garnered all the press, the incred-ibly vast majority of parents agreed with or went along with dress codes.

And the dress codes played an important, appropriate role. They pre-vented disruption of the educational environment, and they supported temperance, moderation (a Stoic virtue). What better lesson in temper-ance is the reasonableness of appearance, manifested in the skirt that is not so abridged as to be above the knee or the male haircut that is not so unwieldly as to reach the shirt collar. Even more, they simply nullify the whole question of appearance. By setting out the parameters, the dress code quells the whole issue as unworthy of further consideration. By setting a speed limit, a state largely ends the discussion of what speed is safe and reasonable (and fuel efficient, at times, at least). By closing the conversation on dress codes, students and the parents can focus on what actually matters, pursuing the education of the student.

A step further in that direction is the school uniform, which the Stoic would also probably endorse unless it included unnecessary frippery and ornamentation, as with the White House guards during the Nixon administration. (After media ridicule, consistent though not identical with Stoic thought, the new, grand uniforms were abandoned, the guards returned to their former attire, and a marching band in Iowa was gifted with a new, regal look.) Mandating a specific uniform allows a school to forego the consideration of individual aspects of student-chosen attire while securing such goals, according to uniform advocates, as the elimination of both distraction and disruption, the leveling of differences emanating from socioeconomic status, and a certain achievement of camaraderie. To the extent that these goals are actually met through uniforms and the prescribed clothing does not violate the limits of moderation, the Stoic educator would have no qualms. Education, unless it somehow strays from the pursuit of wisdom, is a worthy goal, and whatever *reasonably* aids in its pursuit is also worthy. Issues of tattoos, body piercings, profane messaging, extreme hair sculpting, and the rest can be Stoically viewed through the same lens.

But through what lens, more to the point, should educator attire be viewed? The topic is more germane here, as student attire is at least one degree more removed than that of the paraeducator, teacher, or principal. The matter is not terribly complicated. Basically, work clothing for the educator should be practical, durable, and relevant to the task. Thus, different educators will dress differently. An elementary teacher who believes it necessary to work with his children in messy situations, say, on the floor or during art projects, should dress in such a manner to allow such. A physical education teacher would also need to craft her clothing selections to allow for ease of movement and demonstration of athletic and mobility skills.

Beyond these considerations, it would seem that the most important consideration would be the adult educator's need to convey authority. A frequent quip among education's modern reformers is that it never seems to make progress, that 'a time traveler could walk into a classroom in ancient Greece and instantly recognize the familiar aspects of a school.' The unstated assumptions for this criticism include (1) that all other fields of endeavor have changed so much between then and now that a visit to any other institution would leave the traveler feeling like Rip Van Winkle, and (2) that a lack of change in education is necessarily a bad thing. Leaving these aside, one definitely unchanging need in education is for the educator to have authority. One important tool for conveying authority to students is the teacher's appearance, including clothing choices.

And one thing that has definitely changed, at least, since the mid-point of the last century is teacher attire. All women who worked in schools then wore dresses to school. All men wore sport or suit coats and ties. A common bit of advice for the new male teacher was to throw on a tie, as it separated them from the students—a realistic need, especially for high school teachers who were as little as four years older than those they were teaching. It was also something instantly recognized as setting a different tone, an authoritative tone. The Stoic would have no quibble with this. Yes, Zeno wore clothing which provided little in the way of protection from the weather and signaled nothing in the way of authority, but he was teaching adults who were paying for their philosophical studies. Additionally, his behavior, including his clothing, was a demonstration, a direct application, of his teaching for his students. Opulence would have left him looking hypocritical. Neither Seneca nor Marcus Aurelius shied away from clothing suitable to their station, as clothing, for them, was very much a form of communication.

So how, then, should principals, mentors, and well-meaning colleagues approach others, especially those new to the field, about concerns they may have about the attire of paraeducators, teachers, and even principals? For that, a return to Epictetus's conundrum is in order. As that revisit is made, an interesting issue arises. Epictetus, without offending the potential student, is trying to help the student see why his appearance is unnecessarily, even inappropriately, haute couture. In the case of the new teacher, though, the issue is slovenliness. Even so, the same issues apply. Epictetus's student and the novice instructor have crafted an appearance that will interfere with their ability to successfully learn or teach. The goal is to change the other's behavior, which means taking care not to offend them.

Ultimately, the Stoic educator—certainly Epictetus but also, in this example, the principal or colleague offering advice—knows they do not control how the new recruit (as with any human being) will behave. That is entirely within the other's jurisdiction. Thus, only by enlightening them can they hope to have the desired effect. Epictetus cannot demand it, as he does not want to lose his potential student. The principal cannot compel it, at least not these days, in all likelihood, because of teacher shortages or a modern, social distaste for adult dress codes. Thus, this falls into a very similar situation to that of Epictetus. The principal must persuade the rookie to upgrade their attire by decent argument or a sense of knowing the ropes, acting in their best interest. After such a conversation, likely a brief one, some principals will cluck their tongues if a change of behavior does not occur. The Stoic principal, though, will simply drop the matter, comfortable in their clearer understanding that this matter is out of their control.

SUMMARY

Though Zeno of Citium gave an early image of the wardrobe of the Stoics as sparse, plain, threadbare, and even acetic, such a lesson should not be painted with too broad a brush. If a closetful (OK, very much less than full of such Spartan garment) is sufficient for the physical job and social demands of a Stoic, then that is an apt description. If, however, the Stoic is a wealthy businessman and politician, then he can dress like Seneca. If he rules the world's largest empire, he may dress like a king. Student dress codes and even student uniforms can be consistent with Stoic principles if they are instituted for legitimate pedagogical purposes and do not demand unnecessary ornamentation or unreasonable cost. The Stoic educator should dress for school in clothing that is consistent with his or her teaching level and area, while also keeping a close eye on their attire's ability to appropriately separate them from their students and convey a message of authority and expertise. Offering advice to those new to the field on attire and professional appearance should be done so with an eye on the value of persuasion, remembering that another's choices about such things are outside the control of anyone but that individual.

NOTES

1. Epictetus, *The Discourses*, book 3, chapter 1.
2. Epictetus, *The Discourses*, book 3, chapter 1.

Social Skill 8

Do Not Seek the Preferment of Rome . . . or the Central Office

IN BOOK I OF HIS *DISCOURSES*, EPICTETUS IS PORTRAYED IN A SITUATION very common for philosophers of the day, engaging in discussions with his students. Arrian, his student and transcriptionist, states that these exchanges were written down verbatim but also admits that he did so as "far as possible."[1] Court stenographers were in short supply in first- and second-century Rome. Regardless, as Epictetus wrote nothing down, he is what Arrian says he is, and that is impressive.

During World War I, a popular song asked, "How ya gonna keep 'em down on the farm after they've seen Paree?" Visiting a place can change people, especially when it is a place of opulence, not of hard work, a place of temptations not found on home turf. When American doughboys visited Paris on leave, Katie bar the door.

Epictetus reported the same phenomenon for those traveling to Rome and especially for those staying for a bit. They are changed and not for the better. They become accustomed to the luxuries of Rome and even its "work," mistaking the weighing of balances and the balancing of accounts for actual, productive work. And they know they are being misled. For they have told Epictetus that should they manage to escape the miasmic Roman milieu, they will never set foot there again. But then they travel near, and they catch a whiff of *Rome* (as if it were some hypnotizing fragrance worn by a great beauty). Or they receive a letter from Caesar, and they are off and running on one of those roads that all seem to lead to that same place. They lay aside all serious pursuits, such as that of philosophy, for example, and soon the business of the human being is displaced by that of the bean counter, the lickspittle, the animal. "And what else do they do all day long than make up accounts, inquire among themselves, give and take advice about some small quantify of grain, a bit of land, and such kind of profits?"[2]

They sell their souls, their joy, and their tranquility for a handful of barley.

In some sense, this is good news for Stoic educators. Having chosen education as a profession, they have already escaped lesser pursuits. They have done quite the opposite of the "old men," as Epictetus describes them, of Rome. They have placed themselves in a school, a place devoted to the education of youth. Given that Stoics view happiness as emanating from living as a human being is designed to live and that they are social beings with obligations to others, education is a higher calling, one very much aligned with a happy life.

Still, though being an educator provides an environment supportive of resisting the preferments of Rome or simply not being exposed to them much, its protections are neither complete nor foolproof. There are, in fact, a number of education-specific allurements that can take the unwary, not to mention the willing, from the joyful life of the human being in this very social environment, serving the needs of others and meeting their obligations to them. These would include Epictetus's old men and their bean counting, educational honors and awards, and the lure of positions distant or divorced from those they serve.

OLD MEN COUNTING BEANS

Modern motivation theory and experimentation has disrupted what was once believed about what stimulates people in their professional lives. Early on it was accepted canon that people responded to money and money-like incentives (insurance, pensions, etc.). Skinner boxes seemed to support these theories, as rats dutifully pressed on bars to receive pellets. Over time, though, the case for transferring such maxims from the rat to the human employee began to crumble. Today it is generally believed that monetary compensation never satisfies, or if it does, only for a vanishingly tiny sliver of time. It does, however, dissatisfy. In other words, if you pay a person too little, they will be perpetually unhappy (or leave). But once you pay them enough—that is, competitively, at least in the employee's mind—they will no longer be dissatisfied, no longer unhappy. But that doesn't mean they will be happy. Happiness at work tends to come from professional success and autonomy, the ability to do the job according to one's professional judgment.

This certainly rings true, just not for everyone. Modern motivational theory sometimes becomes less descriptive and more aspirational. But it has not rescinded the inclination for, on occasion, almost everyone and, most of the time, at least some to be grasping, focused on what's in it for them. These are people who become overly vitriolic members of negotiating teams, who meet with their state pension representatives several times a year, who constantly question district HR (human resources) people over their pay stubs, and who genuinely believe or at least argue that the only measure of the institution's value of a teacher or other employee is what they pay them.

This creates a serious morale issue for such educators. It invariably destroys their joy. It does so, first, because it always leads to comparisons, and comparisons lead to confirmation bias, the logical error but still real tendency of people to seek out only evidence that affirms their pre-existing beliefs. He who believes that teachers are underpaid will see in the private sector nothing but a sea of entrepreneurs raking in a bonanza and building a massive portfolio. Even though education pays better today than pretty much any time in modern history, the image of the teacher who qualifies for food stamps remains uncorrected. The inventors of the pet rock and the chia pet are cashing in, while those serving children are left in comparative want. This unrealistic view of the world, no matter what evidence exists to the contrary, destroys happiness.

This is also done when, secondly, the whole focus is on compensation. The Stoics would certainly acknowledge that human beings have physical needs and that these needs must be met. But nothing in that realm can bring happiness. Thus, the person who has decided or fallen into believing that the most important thing in life—or even just *a* very important thing in life—is compensation is doomed to unhappiness. Human beings never find happiness, true underlying tranquility, there because that is not how human beings are designed. Scrooge McDuck may find it to be enough to wallow in his acres of lucre in his money bin, but human tycoons find little pleasure in it in the end. It is why Andrew Carnegie built libraries, Rockefeller raised colonial Williamsburg, Bill Gates seeks to eradicate polio, and Elon Musk shoots rockets into space. The great philanthropists are positive proof that money cannot bring joy, at least not the kind of joy the Stoics speak of. Thus, they shift as they age toward service to mankind, an approach consistent with the human design as a social creature with obligations to others.

THE EGO WALL

When a Roman general would return to the capital city after a major victory, for example, fresh off destroying Carthage in battle and salting the earth, the populace would hold a parade for him through the streets of the Eternal City. Frequently, leaders and soldiers from the defeated enemy would be shackled and forced to march before the victor. To be so lauded by the greatest city in the world, to have it placed at one's feet, had to have been dizzying—so much so, in fact, that a practice began of having a slave stand behind the honoree, bending down to the ear of the seated champion, and periodically whispering, "Memento mori." Remember death. It was a pinprick to the balloon of hubris, a way to ground a person even as they were being elevated.

And it is important because nothing can destroy tranquility more quickly than a dramatic, unexpected reversal. It is at the very point of greatest triumph that its fleeting nature, its perishability, must be recognized. It is important, too, for a more utilitarian reason. Flattery leads to ruin. The great Greek tragedies were consumed with this. Take Sophocles's Oedipus trilogy, *Oedipus Rex, Oedipus at Colonus,* and *Antigone.* The main character, Oedipus, sports all the features of a true Greek hero, but his overweening pride makes him grasp for too much, causing him to unknowingly murder his father and marry his mother. Pride does goeth before a fall. Marcus Aurelius, it is believed, had a slave assigned to him to prevent this. Whenever anyone offered the emperor a compliment of any sort, and just imagine how much that must have happened to the emperor of Rome with absolute power, the slave would whisper those now-familiar words, "Memento mori."

It doesn't end there. What educators have discovered in the last several decades but continue to violate with abandon anyway is that providing external rewards for certain behavior or outcomes destroys intrinsic motivation. Provide extra recess time or candy or toys to a child for increasing the amount of reading he does, and the child will very quickly associate the value of reading as the extrinsic rewards it provides, *not* the intrinsic joy of reading. This, too, is a road to ruin, for it will actually decrease the frequency of the desired behavior in the long run. It will only temporarily boost it in the short run, as long as the external benefits are provided. Incentive programs for reading books pose the very real danger of robbing natural readers of their love for doing so. Most educators today know this research, and they have, at least on occasion, experienced the actual results of such. But faced with the need to improve proficiency scores or reduce specific misbehaviors in the classroom or bolster classroom charitable giving for a local food pantry, they time and time again set up a system of rewards. For the time being, the desired behavior goes up, the undesirable behavior goes down, and the perceived value of the activity is drained of all meaning, replaced by a bit of pasta or a plastic toy. It is a poor exchange, a bad bargain.

Are these, then, the same effects for educational honors—being named Teacher of the Year, Most Promising Rookie Principal, or any of the other quickly multiplying recognitions for which educators compete? Perhaps the answer is not for all of them, perhaps not for every educator so recognized, but frequently, it is yes. It has precisely these effects and for precisely the same reasons. Honors of this sort pose the danger of the honored believing their own marketing. Having completed the application in which, like a resume, they are all but forced to exaggerate their accomplishments, provide footage of a suspiciously successful lesson, and secure letters of recommendation written by people who feel compelled to argue their colleague is a virtual combination of Socrates and Christ, they begin to believe it. How can they not? Given the dissonance between believing one is lying (or being lied about) or that they really are this good, they of course select the latter. Well, a lot do.

Then a committee of their colleagues reviews all of the applications and makes a decision in part based on the materials reviewed but also in part based upon other unspoken factors—their sitting on boards of the organization that awards the honor, being a member of the organization, or remaining consistent with the political and social values perceived to be important to public education (but with a tenuous-at-best connection to the skills demonstrated at the fundamental task of teaching or leading). These gated factors are never stated, not publicly at least, but they are known to many who consider applying or being nominated for the honor. But the certificate and announcement don't say, "Teacher of the Year Among Those Who Serve on Our Committee, Toe the Line of Organization Beliefs, Etcetera." They just say, "Teacher of the Year." To the extent such honors are proliferating, spreading to administrators and classified staff and even supportive community members, is not surprising. It is why the Academy Awards now lasts in excess of three hours. People love to be honored, and they love to hand out awards.

This is not harmful in and of itself unless it violates the two principles above, leading to pride, which leads to a fall, and replacing intrinsic rewards with extrinsic ones. The Stoic spurns such awards. Even when he accepts them, he is careful to remind himself—playing the part of the emperor's slave—that they are not, in all likelihood, deserved and that, even if they are deserved, they are irrelevant to the most important aspects of the human being.

Many years ago, a state Teacher of the Year recipient rose to accept his award. As he did so, he reflected on the likelihood that he truly was the very best teacher in the entire state. Then in seemingly unplanned remarks, he said, "I know I'm not the best teacher in the state. Heck, I'm not even the best teacher in my district. Or my school. Come to think of it, I'm not even the best teacher in my hallway at the middle school." And that *was* the truth. There was an English teacher in the same hallway as that math instructor, and she was an outstanding instructor, easily better than him, though he was very, very good. Yet he and his colleagues and administrators joined in the effort to have him so named. On the positive side, at least he knew it. He didn't believe in his own PR. And he said it out loudly, to God and everybody.

So why didn't that English teacher apply for the honor? It is hard to say, but it would be nice to believe that she didn't because she found the recognition and the process that led to it irrelevant to the joy she found in teaching. That tranquility came when she worked with her students, when she watched them achieve a new level of writing skill, when she watched a typically quiet student rise to participate effectively in her classroom Socratic dialogues. It was the intrinsic that led to her joy, while the extrinsic was irrelevant at best, and the process leading to it would be a drain on the intrinsic at worst. What is even worse is that pursuing the honor might replace intrinsic joy with extrinsic pap, might subconsciously convince her that teaching is only valuable if externally recognized.

THE EXPENSIVE PROMOTION

Schools are a workplace notoriously stingy with promotions. While in many corporations, the military, and government agencies, the first job is the lowest rung of a very tall ladder, it is common for a teacher to start, continue, and end their career as . . . a teacher. There are fifteen levels within federal employment, GS-1 through GS-15, and ten steps within each grade. The United States military has four ranks for enlisted personnel, seven for noncommissioned officers, five for warrant officers, and ten for commissioned officers. Private corporations don't have a consistent list of possible jobs and promotions, but in large organizations, they can number in the hundreds.

Education is different. It is just not a place for myriad advancement opportunities. A school district with a couple hundred teachers might have just a dozen administrative posts, and some of these are noneducational (director of facility management, business official, head of food service). It is, frankly, very common for an educator to start their career as a teacher and end it there as well. Raises are small but steady. But if an educator wants to significantly increase their compensation, they basically have to leave the classroom. Changing what they teach or at what level they teach frequently comes with no change in salary other than the small annual increase they would have received anyway. If they want to make more, they have to leave the classroom and join the ranks of administrators.

Even if they do wish to make that switch, the chances are not necessarily good that they will be able to make that happen. There are only so many principalships, and while some believe schools are overadministered, that is only arguably the case if you count staff administrators. A staff administrator includes positions like Title I director, curriculum director, head of ELL (English language learners), and so forth. These administrators guide various departments or initiatives. Line administrators, on the other hand, are those who supervise people, make budgetary decisions, and operate all of the logistics required of an attendance center. Line administrators are, in fact, much less numerous than even basic supervisory theory would argue should exist. Max Weber, the champion of modern organizational theory and especially bureaucracy, said that a supervisor's span of control should be three to five direct reports. Principals commonly have twenty-five and often many more. This creates serious problems of supervision (though it also probably leads to greater autonomy in the profession, a positive though unintended consequence).

It also creates precious few opportunities for promotion from the teacher ranks. It does make one suspicious, though, of the wisdom of such vertical moves. When considering a move into administration, candidates say things like, "I want to serve more kids, have a greater impact than I can in a single classroom." Once they get there, their former peers ask them things like, "So have you ever considered getting back into education?" or "How's the dark side working out for you?" This is not to say that being a building principal cannot be intrinsically rewarding. But finding those moments, those times of changing a child's life for the better, of *teaching*, can be hard to do. Thus, the promotion becomes an expensive one—not expensive in terms of salary. Like the old men of Rome, they get paid more than ever. It is expensive in terms of the meaning of the job.

One of the things school principals are often surprised by, even if they say otherwise, is how much time they spend dealing with students with behavior problems. Cheering a principal up sometimes means reminding them that have 400 or 600 or 1,000 students in their building and that the 15 they deal with on a regular basis are not the entire student body.

The principal and especially the assistant principal are dropped into a silo of disciplinary referrals, budgeting, facility troubleshooting, much of which brings zero tranquility to an educator who previously found their joy in lighting fires among and firing up the imaginations of their students. Soon, having grown accustomed to their higher salary (economists consistently report that people spend a high, essentially fixed percentage of their compensation regardless of how much they make), it is incredibly hard to return to a lower level of spending. *Snap!* go the jaws of the trap into which they have stepped. They have lost the joy they found in teaching but cannot see how they can return to it for financial reasons.

Their promotion is lucrative financially but incredibly expensive in terms of their joy and tranquility in life.

Avoiding the Traps

So how, then, does the Stoic educator avoid these snares? First, they must understand what brings them joy. Fundamentally, this is the same for everyone—acting according to one's human nature as a social being and fulfilling one's duties to others. If they leave the profession for a position that is alien to this social calling or, in particular, harmful to others, they had better be prepared to surrender the joy in life. Thus, they should either not leave the profession or do so only if a position similarly (truly) rewarding can be secured—even if that new position reduces stress, pays better, and gives (gasp!) an hour for lunch.

Second, they must recognize honors, even from fellow educators, for what they are: things outside their control, with often very little congruence with actual success, which pose the very real danger of replacing intrinsic rewards with extrinsic ones, of finding joy only or primarily in the regard in which others hold them. Finally, if they find joy in teaching, they need to carefully and objectively measure the likelihood of finding that same joy in another role. For without that joy, they have made an unwise exchange.

Summary

The Stoic educator does not look to external rewards, the regard of others, or promotion within the profession for the joy and tranquility that he—that everyone—seeks. He has chosen a profession consistent with Stoic ideals and needs only to avoid the mistake of leaving it or minimizing it in order to continue to find that joy. Doing so means clearly recognizing what is probably the main reason he entered the field in the first place—serving others, serving youth. And it means exercising the virtue of wisdom to see that greater salary and perks are not a fair trade for intrinsic joy unless they can be found in another role of service. It means not replacing intrinsic rewards with extrinsic ones like recognitions and honors, as these, if not accepted with a clear head and a critical (some would say cynical) eye, can sop up time in their pursuit instead of tapping into true joy. The danger is especially prevalent when the extrinsic honor threatens to sully the intrinsic reward in even the most sober-minded individuals. And it means not, in pursuit of titles or enhanced compensation, accepting jobs understood to be promotions but which remove him from a genuine teaching role. It means being grounded. The struggle to stay grounded in that which brings true joy is a daily, continuous one, as even the classical Stoics often admitted.

NOTES

1. Epictetus, Introduction by Arrian, *The Discourses*, p. 1.
2. Epictetus, *The Discourses*, book 1.

CHAPTER 11

Social Skill 9

Let Nothing Perturb You, Let Naught Disturb You

THIS MAY SOUND LESS LIKE A STOIC SKILL THAN THE WHOLE POINT OF Stoicism. After all, isn't the goal to have true joy and tranquility in life and, thus, this looks more like the outcome of Stoicism than a skill that leads to it? In truth, it is both. (It is probably also the reason that the Stoic school would lead to the connection with being stoic, emotionally undemonstrative. In truth, if nothing that happens ever disturbs, then few actualized opportunities for emotional display would ever occur.) This is consistent with so many other ventures in life. To be a rich man, invest like one. To be virtuous, display virtue. Being a scholar requires a great deal of study. Once attained, the scholar pursues a great deal of study. Thus, to be a Stoic, remain calm in the face of adversity.

Or, as Seneca says it, "To bear trials with a calm mind robs misfortune of its strength and burden."[1] There is an ongoing debate in the fields of psychology, philosophy, and others about cause and effect. In its simplistic form, one or more things cause another, the effect. Thus, a cook turns on his gas stove, and the soup begins to warm. Yet life is rarely quite so simplistic. Take the example of learning to bat in softball or baseball. Children first learning how will swing with all their might at a pitch or even at a stationary T-ball set, then instantly ease up once the ball is struck or missed. Their batting coach will explain that they need to swing through, to not let up even after they have hit the ball. Well, how can that matter? Once the batter has reached the apogee of his swing, what happens next is irrelevant. Cause cannot follow effect, after all.

But this is a bad conclusion when teaching beginning batters. For the failure to swing through has an impact on the swing from the very start. The rookie is anticipating the end or relaxation of the swing, and that anticipation leads to a checked swing, a swipe at the ball without full power, a tentative, flaccid swat. At this point, it is tempting to engage in an additional conversation about the nature of cause and effect in the first place, saying that such concepts are illusory and also that free will is a myth, that human beings lack the ability to act outside the bounds of what nature and nurture dictate. This is then followed up with the understanding that belief in free will, belief in the human person as a genuine actor, a real difference maker with the ability to choose, has positive effects. In other words, the concept here is that believing in free will is one of the things that dictates behavior, even though free will does not exist. All of that is, in fact, fascinating, but, suffice it to say, the temptation to so engage will not be succumbed to here, at least not anymore than it already has.

Instead, it is only necessary to understand that while effect cannot precede cause, human understanding of effect, by anticipating such, can. Thus, a person desiring the joys pursued by Stoicism can be perceived as desirable, and this desire can lead to acting, in this case, calmly, even before full understanding or rigorous practice of the craft is attained. This would rather ably explain Seneca's offering here. A person receives bad news. A wind storm has split a tree in his yard, and a large limb has fallen on the corner of his house. Even though some would argue that he may simply be overcome by emotion at this point and act accordingly, the truth is he has a choice. He can emote, exclaiming loudly, flailing his arms, smacking his forehead, or he can simply take in the unfortunate news. In today's world, many people would argue for taking the first approach, cautioning against the stoic one as holding in one's feelings, tamping them down to where they will undoubtedly fester and come out in all sorts of nasty manifestations, Freudian and otherwise, and saying that the person is not really dealing with his feelings.

But perhaps what is really happening in such a case is that the person is causing or, at least, exacerbating those feelings. This is explained similarly to these same cause and effect ideas. People generally believe that emotions cause behavior. A person hears of a tragedy, experiences sorrow, and acts upon that emotion by weeping. Yet as many psychologists will explain, behavior often precedes emotion. Witness the light-speed reactions by some people. They seem to begin weeping before the news can have really hit home—certainly not entirely taken in. In such cases, is the weeping the result of the emotion (I feel bad and so will cry) or the the other way around (I am weeping so I must be feeling sad)? Is it possible the stronger connection is the mind/brain sensing a bodily response and developing the emotions consistent with that response? There seems to be a great deal of evidence for this very phenomenon.

Thus, Seneca's notion that one can rob misfortune of its bite simply by responding to it calmly has a reasonable theoretical basis, even if it is one not probably well understood by a long-dead Roman philosopher. It's not an example of faking it until you make it, though that would be another reasonable argument for taking Seneca's advice. Rather, it is a better understanding that the mind and body are in a feedback loop. The nuclear fission reaction is another. The bad news starts the process. The body's trembling continues it, telling the mind that this is indeed terrible news, which then causes additional physical responses. Unless the process is interrupted, a critical mass is achieved and an explosion results.

But isn't this interpretation problematic, given that it flouts long-accepted, modern, enlightened canon that emotions must be released, not sucked up, with an artificial calm? Well, this may be long-accepted, but it is *not always* accepted. Take as one example the poem "If" by Rudyard Kipling:

If you can keep your head when all about you
Are losing theirs and blaming it on you,
If you can trust yourself when all men doubt you,
But make allowance for their doubting too;
If you can wait and not be tired by waiting,
Or being lied about, don't deal in lies,

Or being hated, don't give way to hating,
And yet don't look too good, nor talk too wise:
If you can dream—and not make dreams your master;
If you can think—and not make thoughts your aim;
If you can meet with Triumph and Disaster
And treat those two impostors just the same;
If you can bear to hear the truth you've spoken
Twisted by knaves to make a trap for fools,
Or watch the things you gave your life to, broken,
And stoop and build 'em up with worn-out tools:
If you can make one heap of all your winnings
And risk it on one turn of pitch-and-toss,
And lose, and start again at your beginnings
And never breathe a word about your loss;
If you can force your heart and nerve and sinew
To serve your turn long after they are gone,
And so hold on when there is nothing in you
Except the Will which says to them: "Hold on!"
If you can talk with crowds and keep your virtue,
Or walk with Kings—nor lose the common touch,
If neither foes nor loving friends can hurt you,
If all men count with you, but none too much;
If you can fill the unforgiving minute
With sixty seconds' worth of distance run,
Yours is the Earth and everything that's in it,
And—which is more—you'll be a Man, my son![2]

Notice several salient verses. The first right out of the gate, "If you can keep your head," is precisely what Seneca means by bearing trials with a calm mind. Kipling points to the man (the gender exclusivity is appropriate here, as that was who Kipling was addressing) who can remain calm as the leader and the ideal.

"If you can meet with Triumph and Disaster / And treat those two impostors just the same"; it is a bit hard to imagine a more beautifully and pithily articulated distillation of Stoicism than here. It is not just that the ideal man can take defeat, he can also take victory without reveling in it, without dancing in the end zone or fist pumping in a Facebook post. For they matter the same to him—mostly not—and entirely because they will not impact his long-term joy. Thus, he maintains his short-term tranquility. He remains calm.

There is one more to note: "And lose, and start again at your beginnings / And never breathe a word about your loss"; it's that last part, mostly, of course. The Stoic disdains loss as unimportant to his underlying joy but, to this point, also never laments the loss. He maintains his equanimity amid that loss. He demonstrates his Stoicism through his behavior. This notion should not be entirely novel to the practicing educator. Teachers are trained, at least they should be, to de-escalate situations, to be the adult in the situation. Any number of situations come to mind when considering why the Stoic response, to never become distraught, is best.

9/11

An awareness of current events and a reasonably sophisticated understanding of the world they are and will be living in are important aspects of a child's education. Pursuing these ends is a productive use of instructional time, at least most of the time. 9/11 was probably an exception. Those who were teaching and acting as principal on that day, now more than two decades ago, were faced with a very unique current event. First, it was overwhelming. Second, it was happening in real time. Other than the Challenger disaster, it is tough to think of a truly earth-shattering event that happened during the school day and was widely covered in available media. (Pearl Harbor was attacked on a Sunday. Very few classrooms had televisions on Nov. 22, 1963.) Thus, the attack on the World Trade Center posed an almost unprecedented challenge for educators. How it was handled spread across the entire spectrum of possible responses. In some schools, principals came across the PA systems and ordered all TVs and other available media immediately shut down to student access. In others, no school or district office direction was offered at all. Some teachers took it up as a valid current events lesson, turned on the news coverage, and basically suspended all other content instruction for the day. Others, perhaps out of a need to stay abreast on their own part, kept a television humming with the sound off.

Looking back, all of the reactions had some merit. There was, however, one response that proved problematic. A certain percentage of school people—principals, teachers, paraeducators, and even kitchen staff and custodial—just flat out lost it. They could sense or were told of the magnitude of the loss of life, and they bought into the worst of the fears and the worst-case scenarios being spun by newscasters and on-air consultants. Dirty bombs, widespread terrorist attacks, anthrax-loaded envelope deliveries, and every conceivable modern nightmare were discussed as the inconceivable became conceivable. Students, in part because they were largely much less cognizant of what was really happening, fared better. Where they did not fare as well, though, was where those they looked to for guidance—that is, the authority figures—manifestly struggled, where they broke down in tears, froze up and stared at their televisions, or began loudly accusing whole ethnic and religious groups of culpability, without much sense of proportionality. It was the Stoic educator, the parent in the room, who handled things well, who guided their children through a difficult day without the distraction of strident emotional displays, and who delivered their kids to the parents at the end of a long day so their parents, their first educators, could take over the task of explaining the inexplicable. Even if the classroom teacher did nothing more than maintain a staid decorum, at least the receiving parent didn't face the task of first undoing what had been done badly before taking on helping their child through and toward a hard reality.

COVID

As discussed pretty extensively in the introduction to this book, the COVID pandemic proved to be a crisis with incredibly toxic effects on schools and students. A massive loss of school time; the implementation of a largely untried instructional medium (distance); the deep and abiding controversies among adults and students held vicariously over masks, vaccinations, and other precautions; and a collapse of the age-old commitment to strong attendance in the face of health—physical and mental—concerns sucker punched schools and everyone working within them for more than two years. Those who handled them most ably, those who served students the best, were those who acted in a Stoic fashion. When suddenly politically active students loudly repeated the refrain on masks they were hearing from the parents while their school still required them in any case, the Stoic teacher simply offered, "Yes, but these are the rules, and at least these rules are allowing us to have school in session." Whether they were right or wrong on the issue, it brought calm.

They sidestepped the entire debate, which could not and would not be "won," no matter what position was taken or how deftly wielded were the arguments, understanding that what is beyond one's control is not worth devoting any energy to. What was in their control was getting back to the business of school. When schools became awash in hand sanitizer and classrooms lost their aromas of chalk dust and dry-erase markers in favor of hospital or vaguely alcoholic smells, they set out the pump bottles and quietly ignored them from then on. As plexiglass barriers surrounded student desks and screened off teacher desks—public relation stunts rivaling any Madison Avenue ever conceived as teachers well-understood, with littles ones poking heads around corners and smearing them in opaqueness within minutes of the recitation of the Pledge—they accepted them for just that, nonsense designed to give the impression that something, anything was being done.. Parents needed reassuring, and they accepted this uncontrollable aspect of their classrooms because it brought their children back into their classrooms. They didn't lament them as smacking of government overstep or as pitifully inadequate health measures. Those were the non-Stoics residing on both sides of the educational stalwarts, the Stoics. It was this middle group, these "golden mean-ers," that kept their heads and kept the educational home fires burning.

School Board Meetings

In many ways, this is really just a special case of the item just above—that is, COVID. But it is worth a bit of individual discussion as well because so many school superintendents and board members (probably a smaller percentage, but remember, these are also school "civilians" rather than those in the actual profession), did this well. When they did, they were acting consistently with Stoic principles. They let nothing perturb them.

This is not to say that they were necessarily correct. Whether boards made correct decisions or not is important, but here, it is beside the point.

What is not beside the point is how they reacted to parents and other advocates who came to board meetings, accused them of crimes not publicly charged since the Nuremberg trials, trampled on time limits, and used language that would make Howard Stern blush. How the Stoic board members reacted was with calm. (The masks helped in this sometimes-difficult endeavor.) They did not roll eyes or arch eyebrows. They steadfastly refused to trade expletive for expletive. In the main, they did not attempt to find ways to exclude public participation. Instead, they serenely opened the mikes and listened and listened and listened, saving flinches and angry retorts and draconian measures for that private imagination in which people always know the right barb to offer and can silence antagonists with well-spoken logic in an instant. The perfect handling of these unfortunate events at board meetings by superintendents and board members alike was a composed visage before a calm mind.

STUDENT BEHAVIOR

Much has been said about the droves of teachers and other school people who have fled schools and the profession both during and now, even after, the pandemic. Interestingly, though, some surveys of teachers indicate the COVID malaise is not the number one reason for departures. That honor belongs to student behavior or, rather, misbehavior. A combination of social media encouragement, increased parental support of their children regardless of the offense, and special education "cover" for students with IEPs even extending to violence has made effective teaching a more difficult proposition than in the past. It's not necessarily that the kids have changed so much as the more extreme range of their possible behaviors has been allowed to play out, given these other realities.

Getting a sense of the problem is as easy as accessing social media and tuning into the videos (what isn't recorded these days when everyone is carrying tiny video cameras in their pockets all day, every day?) of students having complete meltdowns, trashing classrooms, threatening and assaulting teachers, and putting fellow students in fear for their lives or physical well-being. This culture that values the extreme lauds people who do what they want and increasingly gives legal protections for misbehavers (through free and appropriate public education in the least restrictive environment for all children who qualify for an IEP), so it is no wonder that schools are experiencing or at least perceiving a major uptick in student misconduct up to and including violence. This is demoralizing on at least two fronts. It disrupts instruction, leaving teachers and paraeducators feeling ineffective and not in control. It leaves principals feeling, even with the best efforts, unsupportive of their staff. It also causes everyone to occasionally fear for their personal safety. Read Maslow for a sense of how demoralizing that can be.

In this case in particular, it might seem as though Stoicism's guidance to not be distraught is less than helpful. But, in fact, it can be. One manifestation of this is in conflict training involving de-escalation. When everyone else is losing their head, the one person who might be able to restore order is the one who does not. The calm response of the Stoic educator serves to de-escalate problematic situations, to modulate voice tone, soften actions, and to generally not buy into the ramping up of a crisis that all those around them are. Short of the various physical restraints that educators are now increasingly being trained in—a certain sign that things are objectively getting tougher out there—it is really the only short-term reaction that is likely to be helpful. In the long-term, another Stoic notion—remembering the communal reality of human nature and actualizing the responsibility to fulfill obligations to others— can be helpful as well by encouraging educators to engage with students, to build positive relationships with them since such connections make student buy-in (or at least compliance) much more likely. Given that, it is necessary to note here that not being perturbed does not mean a flat affect or an unwillingness to engage with others. It simply means being the adult in the room. And how many current social problems are, in fact, caused by too few adults being in the room?

Summary

For a practitioner of Stoicism, not allowing oneself to be disturbed is, oddly, both a Stoic skill and the ultimate goal of the philosophy, to enjoy tranquility in every sense of the word. This is no critique of the philosophy, however but, rather, a practice in it, a fulfillment of it—to pursue joy, to manifest it, even when it is tough. In fact, in an example of ancient philosophy anticipating modern psychologic conclusions, when a person does not respond negatively upon a reversal, when they fail to emote, these very signals communicate back to the person that the problem *can* be handled. It robs the crisis of its bite.

The value of this practice of calm can certainly be seen in the classroom. Take, for example, the teacher who assisted her children through 9/11, which began early in the school day and effectively worsened through it, with a calm demeanor and sent them home to their parents at day's end with, no doubt, many questions but also a sense that they were safe and that the adult world would handle it. During COVID and the many issues it visited upon schools—masks, vaccinations, health regiments, absenteeism—it was the educators who remained composed that helped students and parents alike to accept but not necessarily agree with such measures if it meant the higher goal of getting schooling back on track. Vitriol and condemnations only separated people, while unruffled moves forward helped people to keep navigating an unexpectedly long slog. Finally, as student behaviors have become an increasingly problematic feature in schools, Stoic principles of de-escalation and student engagement have proven to be successful or, at least, more effective than fighting fire with fire, adding hysteria and empty threats, as if these would somehow cool tempers. By acting the Stoic, the educator goes a long way towards reaching Stoic tranquility and offering the same to others.

NOTES
1. Seneca, *Letter from a Stoic*, On the Ficklness of Fortune, letter XCVIII.
2. Kipling, Rudyard. "If- by Rudyard Kipling." Poetry Foundation.

Stoic Skill 10

Control Your Anger—Better Yet, Eliminate It Altogether

WAIT, WASN'T THIS THE TOPIC OF THE LAST CHAPTER? WELL, IT KIND of was. But there are more ways of getting perturbed than just getting angry. And face it, losing one's temper is almost always a mistake. It may be the Stoic's greatest failure, the clearest sign that he has surrendered his joy. Other than intoxicants, it may be Stoic enemy number one. The person who can truly corral their anger, cage up this ogre, and think clearly and rationally about any situation has a much better shot at genuine, deep joy. Most people already know this because they have personally experienced and are now embarrassed about some past behavior, or they have witnessed someone blow their top in such a way that they now feel differently about that person—and not in a good way.

For this self-evident reason, conquering anger is one of the most important skill sets the aspiring Stoic can master—*must* master—or at least get better at. It is not surprising, then, that the ancients identified it as one of the major challenges to face. Seneca wrote a whole treatise on it, *On Anger.* It is definitely worth a read. It also reflects a genuine understanding of human nature because it includes corrective advice on how to prevent anger but also suggestions on how to avoid doing evil *when angry.*

Nevertheless, the master on bringing anger to healing is the emperor Marcus Aurelius. In his *Meditations,* book 11:18, he offers ten quite useful thoughts on the human reality of anger. Each of these is worth serious consideration, especially as they have related to the reality of the modern educator. Well before that, though, in book 2, the emperor offers a wonderful overview and perhaps his most recognized passage:

> Begin the morning by saying to yourself, I shall meet with the busybody, the
> Ungrateful, arrogant, deceitful, envious, unsocial.[1]

Not to dabble in cynicism, but this could easily qualify as an apt description of at least most classroom sections in schools throughout the world. To continue, the emperor says the following:

> All these things happen to them by reason of their ignorance of what is good and
> evil. But I who have seen the nature of the good that it is beautiful, and of the
> bad that it is ugly, and the nature of him who does wrong, that it is akin to mine, not
> only of the same blood or seed, but that it participates in the same intelligence and
> the same portion of divinity, I can neither be harmed by any of them, or no one can
> fix on me what is ugly, nor can I be angry with my brother, or hate him. For we
> are made for cooperation, like feet, like hands, like eyelids, like the rows of the upper
> and lower teeth. To act against one another then is contrary to nature; and it is
> acting against one another to be vexed and to turn away.[2]

People are fraught with every manner and disorder and disagreeableness. They do so because they don't know any better. But the Stoic does know better, and he understands that getting angry or hating others is not only useless, it violates the duties he has to others. The applications to the Stoic educator are obvious. Every teacher understands this, at least in their heart.

The emperor is certainly off to a good start, especially as to his relevance to education. Now he turns, nine books later, to the specifics, numbered here and in the *Meditations* (but a bit differently).[3]

1. First, what is my relation to men; we are made for one another; or, in another view, I was made to be set over them, as a ram over a flock or a bull over a herd.

This is the Stoic understanding that all people have obligations to others that they must fulfill if they are to be happy. The principal, the teacher, and the paraeducator are, in the school, indeed set over their students. When faced with classroom situations in which anger is a likely result, the Stoic educator remembers his or her obligation to the students, considers the ineffectiveness of the response made in anger, and returns to his or her position as servant leader, the notion that the leader leads best when he or she serve others—in this case, students.

2. Second, consider how men are at table, in bed, and so forth; and particularly, under what compulsions they are with respect to opinions; and as to their acts, consider with what pride they do what they do.

When people become angry with others, they tend to narrow their focus, narrowing it to the point where the person, in their mind, is entirely that thing or act or fault that has caused them to be angry. They cannot see the whole person. To dispel anger, consider the person as a whole, and anger may well dissipate. This is especially a problem for building principals. This poor lot gets to know a small percentage of the student body very well because this percentage is sent repeatedly to their office. It becomes hard not to conceive of this student as the attendance problem; that student, the insubordinate one; another, the mouthy one. This leads to anger. The headmaster who can remind herself of something the child does well or even a single incident in which they showed consideration (e.g., opening a door for someone, standing up for a friend) can flesh out the child standing once again at his door.

3. Third, that if men do rightly what they do, we ought not to be displeased; but if they do not right, it is plain that they do so involuntarily and in ignorance. For as every soul is unwillingly deprived of truth, so also it is unwillingly deprived of the power of behaving to each man according to his deserts. Accordingly, men are pained when they are called unjust, ungrateful, and greedy, or charged with behaving wrongfully to their neighbors.

When someone becomes angry with another, it is typically because they believe they have done something wrong—not always, of course, since sometimes people say, "Well, I understand that they had to do what they did, but I don't like the way they went about it." The Stoic disagrees. As the emperor notes, "If men do rightly what they do," others should not be angry with them.[4] They did the right thing. Even if they did the wrong thing, it is likely out of ignorance of just what the right thing to do was, or they did it involuntarily. In those cases, there is no cause for anger either. When English teachers argue over the merits of the science-of-reading approach vs. the balanced-reading approach, either might be right, and even the incorrect one is still probably acting out of good intentions. Thus, anger is not warranted. If a student sent to the office "beats the office referral back to the classroom" (i.e., received no noticeable punishment whatsoever), rather than becoming angry with the principal, the teacher's better option is to assume the boss was right or that punishment occurred but hasn't yet been communicated or that, perhaps, he didn't fully understand the situation. And if all of these possible sources of anger between adult personnel should be discounted, how much more should anger be dissuaded by a teacher for a student. Perhaps he has been raised to display behavior that in the school setting appears insubordinate but at home is perfectly acceptable. Such behavior should be corrected, of course, but if it leads the teacher to anger, that is problematic and, in all likelihood, counterproductive.

4. Fourth, consider that you also do many things wrong, that you are a man like others; and even if you abstain from certain faults, you still have the disposition to commit them, though either through cowardice, or concern for reputation, or some such mean motive, you refrain from wrongdoing.

Those free from sin should cast the first stone. The emperor is pointing out that people often get angry with others over some of the same things they do themselves. The person out for a leisurely Sunday drive is the same one who excoriates others for not getting out of the way when he is in a hurry. The father furious with his kids for leaving the house a mess can't seem to place his own dirty clothes in the hamper or wipe down the inside of the microwave when he's had a boil over. And when he does keep things tidy, it is more because he's afraid the kids will catch him in hypocrisy or because he's afraid of his spouse's wrath. How much better is the person who behaves out of poor motives (rather than just willingly doing the right thing) than the one who just leaves the toilet seat up?

It is sometimes said in the classroom that the teachers who were the teacher's pet with a perfect GPA and spotless desk/locker are at a distinct disadvantage. They have no memory of what they did and why they did it. Homework and tests were always a breeze. When they first meet students for whom none of this is second nature, they cannot imagine the problem. Disbelief turns to anger in a very short period of time. This simply means they need to translate their understanding of their students' failing to some failings of their own in a different part of life. Getting angry with students who are late turning in work, who blurt out in the classroom, or who are deliberately noncompliant is not a recipe for correcting behavior. It is, instead, a recipe for a worsening relationship between teacher and student and for little chance of corrective actions by the student. Understanding failures on the student's part through the lens of the teacher's own inadequacies elsewhere dispels that anger and creates a platform in which improvement is possible, without impairing prospects for long-term progress.

5. Fifth, consider that you do not even know whether men are doing wrong or not, for many things are done with a certain reference to circumstances. In short, a man must learn a great deal to enable him to pass a correct judgment on another man's acts.

Marcus Aurelius put his finger on the attribution bias centuries before the moderns discovered it. The attribution bias is the tendency for people to ascribe flawed motivations for other's misbehavior while recognizing extenuating circumstances for the same behavior in themselves. A man sees someone careening down a city street at breakneck speed and assumes he is just some jerk with no regard for the health and safety of others. He is practically a sociopath. Two days later, when he is shooting down the same street well in excess of the posted speed limits in order to not be late for work, he excuses any culpability on his own part because he is trying to be punctual, he doesn't want to keep others waiting, and no one could have foreseen the dog getting off his leash that morning, which was what made him late in the first place. He has every motivation to let himself off the hook, along with the situational knowledge for "evidence." He knows nothing about the other guy and so just assumes the worst. He attributes to him the basest of motivations, even underlying character flaws, without much in the way of reflection.

A paraeducator has been assigned a new student to work with in order to catch them up from the learning loss they experienced during COVID. This is a student who, even before the pandemic, was always just on the cusp of failure but somehow managed to stay afloat. COVID and virtual schooling sank her. The school has now dedicated funding and personnel to ensuring that she is not the latest educational victim of the pandemic. Her teacher prepares on-point interventions, and the para throws herself into her work, enthusiastically developing these into fun activities and building a positive, professional relationship with the girl. For her part, the student engages very little, completes some of the work only when the para stays on her, and makes very little progress as a result. In their after-school meetings, the teacher and assistant lament the student's lack of motivation. "She's just flat-out lazy." "She doesn't care." "I don't know why we're killing ourselves to get her caught up when she clearly doesn't care." Discouragement on their part, reflecting back one upon the other, quickly leads to anger with the girl. What they see is a lazy, unappreciative teenager who can't be bothered with her own education. What they don't see is a kid with an undeveloped sense of the connection between her work and her likelihood of graduating, a perplexity over this sudden demand for her to put in extra work when her past efforts kept things in place, and a view of education as really not all that relevant, as picked up from parents and siblings. A misunderstanding of the motivations of the student is leading her teacher and helper to increasing levels of anger. Anger is getting them nowhere. They have a problem to be solved, not a brat to be castigated and left to fend for herself.

6. Sixth, consider when you are vexed or grieved that man's life is only a moment, and after a short time we all lie stretched in death.

This argument against anger doesn't require much in the way of explanation. It's the old what- difference-is-this-going-to-make-in-a-hundred-years view. It is important to remember, though, what the emperor isn't saying. He isn't saying that nothing without enormous importance is a waste of time. (Though, for the sake of argument, this might have actually been reasonable thinking for a man in charge of the Roman Empire. His priorities would have been quelling social unrest, defending the borders from pagan incursions, and foiling rivals for his throne. Anything but these might well have been considered a waste of time.)

What he is saying, instead, is that getting angry over small potatoes is wasted emotion and squandered effort. Instead, go about solving problems through productive means. The person finding themselves getting angry over things can quell that furor by taking the long view. Life is short, and spending it angry is a lousy way to spend the little time that is actually available. This is a way to escape anger.

Successful long-term teachers all tend to take this view. They have seen scores of children in their classrooms who have failed to show up literally and metaphorically, who have disrupted class, and who have wasted incredible potential by doing absolutely nothing to capitalize on it. There had to have been times when this left them incredibly infuriated. But upon reflection, they must have also noticed that they were the only one caring. The child clearly didn't care. The parents, caring or not, had surrendered the field, as "we can't do a thing with her." This isn't the first example of such a waste, and it wouldn't be the last. Getting her dander up wasn't going to change anything in the long run. This isn't the same thing as a teacher giving up or becoming burned out. It is, instead, a mature understanding that this one missed opportunity was something that would happen in a long career. This cools what would be an understandably angry response and also a response that would keep a good teacher working with her students rather than leaving the profession in exasperation.

7. Seventh, that it is not men's acts which disturb us, for those acts have their foundation in men's ruling principles, but it is our own opinions regarding them. Take away these opinions then, and resolve to dismiss your judgment about an act as if it were something grievous, and your anger is gone.

Stoics are very big on the difference between events and how one interprets such events. It is a bit like the notion of sense data. Human beings receive input from the physical world through a multitude of senses—hearing, seeing, tasting, proprioception, and so forth. This does not necessarily mean, though, that human sense organs accurately transmit conceptions of those physical realities to the human brain. Philosophers have spent centuries trying to get a handle on the distinction between perceived and actual reality out there. It is important because science is based upon data collection, and data is collected through the senses. If the senses are somehow fundamentally flawed or even if it is impossible to really tell if they are accurate monitors or not, then science is thrown into question. (One simple illustration of this issue is the difference between human and canine perceptions of the world. People very much *see* the world. Their dogs *smell* it. Imagine just how that must color—or perfume?—the perception of reality.)

If even basic sense data is suspect, how much more then is the perception of the acts of others? Such acts have to first be sensed; then the intentions behind them, interpreted; then the accuracy of the third person, determined understanding those intentions. This is a process more complicated by magnitudes than simply seeing an object, smelling an odor, or hearing a sound. Anger occurs when the third person interprets them in such a way that they are offended by the act as intended, according to their interpretation. Avoiding the anger is as simple as disregarding that final interpretation. If a person known and regarded by another walks into a restaurant, peers in his or her direction, and then walks away without comment, the second person may feel snubbed. One solution, as per no. five—that is, attribution error—is to decide that he may have been in a hurry, his glasses were fogged from the shift to the heated air indoors, or that he simply overlooked their table. (Misinterpreting the actions of others seem to be the basis of 90 percent of sitcoms.)

Another solution, though, is to rob the situation of its interpersonal content. Yes, the person walked in. Yes, they peered in their direction. Yes, they walked away without any sort of acknowledgment. But the one supposedly snubbed has a choice. They can accept what happened but decide to draw no conclusion from it, since to do is to cause anger. Or they can decide to go with their opinions and become angry. Since anger disrupts the tranquility of that person, why go there? Why not instead cleanse the situation of its emotional impact by simply ignoring that aspect of it? In some ways this is an especially interesting argument for Marcus Aurelius to make. Political leaders are often quite careful about not tolerating disrespect in their presence. If anything, such a position was far more important to ancient leaders, who interpreted indignities to be swipes at both their person and the position, sometimes even their purported divinity. Modern leaders are more likely to protect—or at least say they are concerned solely about—their office. In any case, if this Roman emperor could find a way to simply block anger by dismissing interpretations of disrespect, those not carrying such obligations should find the technique far easier to utilize.

That good teachers and principals already do this should be a signal to the Stoic educator that wielding this weapon is worthwhile. When a student is behaving well, such behavior can be reinforced by supportive comments and positive regard. (Actual rewards will invite the replacement of intrinsic motivation with extrinsic, entirely the wrong direction.) But *catching* a particularly dysfunctional student—the kind principals are tempted to give punch cards for their number of office visits—can be difficult. After all, such a student is not the only one in the classroom, and problematic behavior always sticks out like a sore thumb in a way that the digits of acceptable behavior don't. The question, then, becomes how to deal with the unfortunate behavior of such a student when it occurs.

Even though educators know better—even a cold fish like B. F. Skinner with all his rodent friends knew it—they almost invariably pivot to punishment. Punishment can be defined as the levying of some disliked consequence on a student and might include a ruler crack across the knuckles and spanking (in the old days) or loss of recess, a detention, and a suspension (both in and out of school) these days. The problem with punishment is that it tends to destroy what relationship had existed and create unintended dysfunctional reactions. Pride and showing off for peers (hence the admonition to not confront students in front of their classmates) escalate the student's misbehaviors. Unless the educator is trying to intensify things in order to, say, remove a student, something most educators consider reprehensible but was a fairly common practice a half century and more ago, punishment is largely counterproductive.

What remains, then, is extinction, the lack of any reward or even any consequence at all in response to an undesirable behavior, pretty much ignoring the behavior. This can be easier said than done, of course, but the idea is to take the fun out of the misbehavior for the student by not reacting. There is no reward but no punishment either. It is also a means of de-escalating behavior. The student acts up and the teacher speaks to them calmly, with little or no emotion, and certainly no judgment in their voice. The short-term goal is to lower the tension in the room, to talk the student down, and to get the classroom back into a place where teaching can occur. The long-term goal is to extinguish the behavior.

Doing so requires the educator to either *have* no anger at their behavior or the child or, at least, to *evince* no anger. It is just what Marcus Aurelius is describing, taking the emotion out of the situation and reaching a point where no anger is felt because no anger is warranted. Of course, this is easier said than done, and educators even take lessons in de-escalation. But emotional responses, at least for the Stoic, are a choice like any other. Remove the emotion, remove the anger, and the situation becomes manageable. Tranquility is achieved.

8. Eighth, consider how much more pain is brought on us by the anger and vexation caused by such acts than by the acts themselves, at which we are angry and vexed.

There are people in this world who have never faced a crisis they couldn't make worse. It's true today, and apparently, it was also true during the reign of Marcus Aurelius. These people should not enter the education profession, at least not today. If you need an illustration of this particular piece of advice, just go online and find one of the million videos of people being stopped by law enforcement who, when faced with a ticket or summons, manage to parlay that into a physical altercation with police, an arrest, or jail time—sometimes all three. Or just think of any *Andy Griffith* episode involving Barney Fife.

The much more common manifestation of this in the classroom is the student who makes a misbehavior mountain out of a minor infraction molehill. Teachers can help ameliorate such situations by de-escalating student behavior. They cannot, however, eliminate them altogether because of another Stoic principle, the understanding that one can control only one's own decisions. There are going to be outbursts and cheating and insubordination and every other form of misbehavior from gum chewing to fighting, and the teacher cannot prevent all of that through de-escalation. What they can control, though, is their response to it.

The emperor is pointing out here that inserting anger and that lovely word *vexation* into situations will never improve things. In fact, it will make them worse. Some students make it their personal goal to get the teacher's goat. Others manage it without even intending it. The teacher who takes the bait has lost. The one who does so repeatedly is probably not long for the profession. This advice works on two levels. First, any educator who brings anger to the crisis has, prima facie, allowed their tranquility to be disrupted and failed in the fundamental Stoic goal. Second, because anger will only make things worse, they have created for themselves, over and above the lost temper, a larger crisis and worse outcomes. This is a lose-lose. Remove the temper and the educator can begin working toward an actual solution or, at least, keep the problem small.

9. Ninth, consider that benevolence is invincible if it be genuine, and not merely an affected smile and playing a part. For what will the most violent man do to you, if you continue to be of a benevolent disposition towards him and, as opportunity offers, gently admonish him and calmly correct his errors at the very time he is trying to do you harm, saying "Not so my child. We are constituted by nature for something else; I shall certainly not be injured, but you are injuring yourself, my child." And show him with gentle tact and by general principles that this is so, and that even bees do not as he does, nor any animals which are formed by nature to be gregarious. And do this neither with any double meaning, nor in the way of reproach, but affectionately and without rancor in your soul; and not as if you were lecturing him, or to show off before others, but quietly in his own ear, even if others are present."

More than any of the others, this advice seems particularly aimed at school people. One of the criticisms of de-escalation approaches to student behavior (and, yes, student behavior has been the focus here, but the same principles can apply to difficult encounters with parents, supervisors, and others) is that it lets students off the hook. Does it really make sense to "ignore" the behavior? No, it doesn't, and the emperor makes it clear here. He isn't saying to just ignore the outrageous behaviors of others. He specifically recommends correcting the poor behavior of others. (Notice the important word "calm," though.) "[A]s opportunity offers," he says, intervene, even "admonish."[5] This is precisely the expectation of educators. As a principal de-escalates the student who is having a meltdown, he is using calm, nonjudgmental language for the short-term but isn't (or shouldn't be) excusing the behavior. Once calm is restored, gentle, constructive admonishment begins, along with a healthy dose of problem solving.

Doing that both short-term and long-term requires the removal of any anger ("without rancor in your soul") in the admonisher. Notice what else needs to be removed. "And do this neither with any double meaning, not in the way of reproach . . . not as if you were lecturing him, or to show off before others."[6] These, too, are manifestations of anger. The educator trying to help a student improve their behavior needs to eliminate all sarcasm and snarkiness from their words. This should seem like a "duh" moment. Who doesn't know that? But sarcasm can be a hard habit to break. For some people it is almost second nature. But it is corrosive, especially to teenagers who have sometimes only recently mastered the art and the understanding of it. And it is particularly corrosive to relationships. It does not encourage better behavior. It challenges the student's pride and, thereby, escalates the issue, in all likelihood. He adds the advice to admonish others without lecturing and to do so privately, not in front of others. What seems remarkable in all of this is that this second-century Roman emperor can give advice that is so spot-on. Educators who want to improve behavior, to help their students, speak with them in a respectful voice as they would speak to the adult they are becoming, and they do so away from others so that the student loses the audience and the need to perform that comes with it. Modern educators sometimes think such techniques are the latest things, but they are not, unless one considers the latest thing to be eighteen hundred years old.

10. But if you will, receive also a tenth gift from Apollo, leader of the Muses, and it is this: that to expect bad men not to do wrong is madness, for he who expects this desires an impossibility. But to allow men to behave evilly to each other, and to expect them to do you any wrong is irrational and tyrannical.

Some educators, usually unconsciously, believe that just writing their teacher name on the whiteboard or putting their principal nameplate on their door will instantly bring respect and compliance from students. This is usually because that is precisely how it affected them when they were in school. They obeyed every directive from their teacher and couldn't imagine being sent to the principal's office. How unfair, then, that they now face classrooms where at least some of the students were not trained to respect their teacher and fear their principal. The sooner they understand reality, the better. "To expect bad men not to do wrong is madness" can quickly be translated into "to expect young people to not occasionally step over the line, way over in some cases, is madness." Every teacher has discipline problems. If every principal didn't have office referrals, superintendents would stop hiring a bunch of them. Student misbehavior is a fact of school life. (Unfortunate behavior among all educators is also a fact of life, and the same principles apply.)

Why is it so important for educators to accept this reality? This is so for several reasons. First, if they don't understand this, they won't prepare for it. And they need to prepare for it. The teacher's pet who becomes a teacher is woefully unprepared for the realities of their first day in their first classroom. Second, if they fail to understand this, they may inaccurately decide that they are a failure. Their naïve expectation that all students will behave for them will very quickly be dispelled. If, though, they internalize that, they may simply decide they are a poor teacher or that this isn't the job for them, and education loses someone who could be a wonderful teacher—once their toolkit has a few more tools in it. Reaching the understanding that human nature can be a treacherous thing means that the teacher can respond to such as, if not positive, at least normal, and leave the anger behind. Doing that will bring more positive results for students and more joyful results for those who teach them.

Summary

Anger is a special case of the Stoic wish to avoid having their tranquility disrupted. It is also, perhaps, the most frequent one. For this reason, Emperor Marcus Aurelius offers ten reflections on anger and how to rid oneself of it. All ten have useful applications to the educational profession and those who work in it. The ten can be summarized as follows:

1. Stoics have natural obligations to others, and anger interferes with meeting them.

2. People are more than their poor behaviors, and anger should be tempered by this understanding.

3. Anger at people doing the right thing is misplaced. Anger at people doing the wrong thing is undeserved because they likely acted out of ignorance or acted involuntarily.

4. When a person becomes angry with another, they overlook their own misbehavior or the self-interested—that is, hardly valorous—reasons for their correct behavior.

5. Given that people consider their own misbehavior as occurring under extenuating circumstances but other's misbehavior as a fundamental character flaw (attribution bias), anger at those others is unfair and unseemly.

6. Given the brevity of life, anger at most offenses is simply unwarranted.

7. Since anger actually arises from the person's opinion of the misbehavior, stop formulating such opinions, and the anger will not occur.

8. Anger often causes more problems than the external source of the anger. Don't add to the problem.

9. Admonishing or correcting others is an obligation, but doing so with anger—and all of its fellow travelers (sarcasm, snarkiness, and boasting)—is ineffective and likely counterproductive.

10. Accept that human nature is such that most or all people will misbehave. Given that, what is the use of anger? One might as well angrily rail against the coming in or going out of the tide.

The emperor's specific advice (see no. nine in particular) seems to foreshadow advice and management techniques for school people by almost two millennia. No wonder he has a consistent presence on history's exceedingly short list of philosopher kings!

NOTES

1. Marcus Aurelius, *Meditations*, book II, chapter 1.
2. Marcus Aurelius, *Meditations*, book II, chapter 1.
3. Marcus Aurelius, *Meditations*, book XI, chapter 18.
4. Marcus Aurelius, *Meditations*, book XI, chapter 18.
5. Marcus Aurelius, *Meditations*, book XI, chapter 18.
6. Marcus Aurelius, *Meditations*, book XI, chapter 18.

CHAPTER 13

Stoic Skill 11

Ask Not "Why Me?" but "Why Not Me?"

IN THE MODERN WORLD, PERHAPS IN PART BECAUSE OF ADVANCES IN medicine (vaccinations, treatments, nutrition), safety engineering, and workplace protections, among others, people are often aghast at life's reversals. After a long, productive, and healthy life, a man is struck by cancer and feels betrayed by this unexpected malady. A woman bemoans her fate when it is her child who dies in an automobile accident, even with the safeguards of car seats, air bags, and automobile crash testing. A young man is blindsided by the loss of his dream job due to corporate restructuring. A young woman is stunned to find she is unable to conceive a child with her husband. And all of these respond with the same lament, "Why me?"

The Stoic does his best to not react in this way. It is not *necessarily* because he believes in an afterlife (though he may) or believes losses to be mere trifles or that he participates in denial, one of Kubler-Ross's stages of grief. (Grief is not limited to feelings over death but, in truth, any significant loss.) Frankly, the Stoic is too hardheaded for that. Instead, the Stoic rejects the specialness implied by the question, "Why me?" Because tragedy and reversal are part of the human condition, everyone is vulnerable to those possibilities. It is a part of life. Thus, the better question is "Why not me?" This would be perhaps, then, the first means the Stoic would employ for dealing with loss. There are a number of others as well.

To illustrate these, consider three examples of losses for the professional educator:

The assignment to an elementary school teacher of an "impossible" class of students. Due to unexpected student numbers at the elementary school at which she teaches, her normal class size has jumped from twenty-two to twenty-seven. A new demographic has arrived as well, including six students who speak no English. Seven of her students have individualized education programs, each requiring additional investments of time in planning and attending IEP meetings. Two of these students have serious compliance or emotional disorders. In one case, the district has offered differential placement because of the possibility of real violence, but the parents have refused it, arguing the guarantee of their child's education in the least restrictive environment—a federal, legal requirement.

Attacks at the highest levels on a middle school teacher by the parents of one of her students. In the middle of the school year, this English teacher assigned a failing grade to an eighth grader's essay because it did not follow proper form. The teacher offered the opportunity for the child to rewrite the paper for partial credit, but the student missed the deadline. The parents were unconcerned until they realized this put their child on the failing list, making him ineligible to play basketball for two weeks. The parents then demanded the opportunity for their son to rewrite the essay. The teacher refused since the deadline had been missed and felt the student needed to take responsibility for his work or lack thereof. The parents called her every name in the book, declaring they would have her job for this. They went next to the principal, who refused to change the child's grade, as he didn't believe in changing a teacher's mark, though leaving the parents with the impression, warranted or unwarranted, that he felt the teacher was being overly strict. When the superintendent's office similarly declined to change the grade or offer an extension, they appeared at the public input section of the school board meeting and loudly ridiculed the teacher by name over the board chair's attempts to gavel them down. The parents initiated a formal complaint process through school board policy and lodged an ethics complaint with the state department of education, which had no choice but to review the matter, as they had no discretion to decline. They wrote letters to the editor of the local newspaper and, when they refused to print it, dove into social media, demanding that the teacher be fired. The teacher found herself spending hours almost everyday defending herself from such accusations on so many levels, in addition to members of the public who knew nothing of the case but believed that where there's smoke, there's fire. The combination of the stress, time spent on responding, and the normal but extensive time demands of grading compositions left her exhausted at the end of most days.

A high school teacher's contract termination. A new principal finds the teaching methods of a fifteen-year chemistry teacher to be outdated and out of step with the newest research on effective teaching. The instructor believes his methods are indeed effective and provides demonstrations and research on his views during the evaluation conference. The principal is unconvinced. By the end of the year, after two more disappointing evaluations, the principal hands the teacher a set of requirements for improving his pedagogy, noting at the bottom that if improvements are not seen in the following year, contract termination is a distinct possibility. Just cause for termination in their state is such that the threat is real. The teacher spends the ensuing summer working on new teaching techniques, those recommended by his principal, and he masters them. In the fall, he revises his lesson plans to accommodate the new teaching style. He receives a more positive evaluation that fall. By Thanksgiving, however, he can see that his new methods are resulting in lower—in some cases, much lower—mastery of the content by students. He shows these results to his principal, but the administrator is unswayed. The teacher realizes he cannot allow his situation to lead to deficient learning for his students and so returns to his former tried-and-true methods. In March, he is notified that his contract will not be renewed for the subsequent year. By June, he is walking out of school with a cardboard box filled with the contents of his tan, maple desk.

"Why Not Me?"

In the first example, the teacher employing this Stoic technique simply decides not to feel put upon by her imposing circumstance. Occasionally, all teachers receive a tough class. She should expect no different for herself. In the second example of the challenging parents, the teacher decides that one of the realities of modern schooling is unsupportive, even exasperating parents, and that this year is her turn. In the example of the chemistry teacher, he considers his options—worsen his teaching skills and hurt his students' learning or get fired. "Hey," he reasons, "people get fired even when they really don't deserve it. Why should I be any different?"

BE PREPARED

Seneca wrote extensively on the topic of grief. He even entered into epistolary counseling sessions with prominent Roman citizens who were drowning in grief in order to help them find their way to dry land. But these were largely after-the-fact measures. A more proactive approach to such is negative visualization, as described in chapter 3. Epictetus believed in it so strongly that he even went there, to that place which instills fear and despair in the hearts of parents.

"If you are kissing your child . . . , say that it is a human being (a mortal) whom you are kissing, for thus when they die, you will not be disturbed."[1]

That is a bridge too far for most, but given that it is the tragedy which would be most devastating, it is arguably the one most important to prepare for. The larger point, though, is that if negative visualization can prepare people for this kind of tragedy, it can certainly prepare them for lesser, though significant, reversals in their personal or professional life.

Thus, in example one, the elementary teacher should begin reflecting now on the possibility that she will be assigned a challenging class later, at some point in her career. Walking through the steps of such a process, one finds at least two positive outcomes are likely. First, she will become emotionally ready for it, which may well take away much of the sting if and when it happens. Second, unless she is truly a doom-and-gloom fatalist, she will also consider ways of positively handling such a situation, perhaps taking a beginning course in another language, meeting the requirements of her next teaching certificate renewal through a course on acceptable restraint measures, and reading up on the research on class size and student performance. Given sufficient time and space to so reflect, such an eventuality might start to look manageable.

Example two, the middle school teacher with the challenging parents, can also be addressed through negative visualization. Imagining such a process is important because, for most teachers, though they've had helicopter parents and uninvolved parents and (name your poison here) parents, this would be a horse of a different color. Yes, it would be terrible and scary (even though unlikely to the rather frightening extent described here), but finally getting a look at the monster in a favorite horror movie often has the effect of lowering fears. Imagining parents like these may very well do the same. They would also provide a time to prepare logistically. A bit of training in methods of chunking aspects of life—such that the terrible ones don't bleed over into everything else—might be in order. Is the instructor aware that in most places, teachers are not considered *public persons*, and so slander and libel relief can be sought? Is she aware that if this district's policies are like most, personnel cannot be criticized in public board meetings, and it is the district's responsibility to enforce that to the extent possible, or that student performance is covered by privacy laws, but this is less so for adults? This is not to suggest any sort of legal or personal strategy in a situation like this, but some reading well in advance might be worthwhile. Forewarned—even when the warning comes from within—is forearmed.

Example three, the high school chemistry teacher facing contract termination, can also benefit from such preparation. Superintendents, it was noted earlier, come in two types: those that have been fired and those that are going to get fired. Understanding that—perhaps it is an understanding that anyone working for a living would benefit from—should take out some of the sting. Knowing the potential reduces the impact when it is actualized. As for more practical preparation, the teacher could investigate their just cause rights in their state or their employee master agreement. Or they could do one better and maybe annually click on the resume icon in their personal folders and polish that document up. Chemistry teachers are hard to come by.

MISFORTUNE STRENGTHENS.

"The true man is revealed in difficult times. So, when trouble comes, think of yourself as a wrestler whom God, like a trainer, has paired with a tough young buck. For what purpose? To turn you into Olympic-class material."[2]

"What would have become of Hercules, do you think, if there had been no lion, hydra, stag, or boar—and no savage criminals to rid the world of? What would he have done in the absence of such challenges? Obviously, he would have just rolled over in bed and gone back to sleep. So by snoring his life away in luxury and comfort, he never would have developed into the mighty Hercules."[3]

Isn't it interesting that people often try to avoid that which is good for them? A few decades ago, it was not unheard of for schools to hold vaccinations clinics. The story is told of an elementary school providing such to its students for a novel disease strain. Parents had signed permission slips, but most students were oblivious. On the day of the jabbing, it seems, a group of third graders lined up in the hallways and stepped forward one by one. Those in front were the only ones who could see what was going on. As one of those realized what was happening, he turned around, cupped his hands around his mouth, and shouted to his classmates, "They're giving shots!"

Such antics are laughable because children sometimes try so hard to avoid what is best for them. Adults do the very same. Many World War II veterans will tell you they didn't want to go off and fight the Axis powers, but having survived it, they found the experience brought incredible meaning to their lives. Whatever else they managed to accomplish in life, they—and 4 million of their buddies—saved the world. It's not bad to have that in the back pocket at age twenty-one. The rest of life probably looked easy. It did because they had developed a mettle and a resilience that could handle anything. That is the power of the negative experience, the reversal. It builds up the person who fights their way through it.

If the elementary teacher really believed this, they might well hope for the kind of classroom that they had before shunned. What a boot camp experience to figure out how to work with children who speak no English, who struggle so mightily with self-control. In a past still within the memories of retired teachers out there are class sizes far larger than today. How did they manage it? What kind of skills did they have to cultivate? Would anyone build such assets if they weren't forced to do so? That middle school teacher may have some of the skills necessary to work with parents who have genuinely gone around the bend, but certainly not all. Wouldn't it be interesting if teachers—and a few do—drew up resumes that included not just college degrees and teaching experience (years, grade levels, locations) but also specific skill sets? Such a list might include the ability to individualize instruction, manage IEPs of specific disabilities in the classroom, or teach with discovery methods. What sort of skills sets might such parents require? Listing them would demonstrate the kind of progress an otherwise just plain negative experience might provide. Like those veterans, working through such a process would leave an indelible sense of accomplishment.

And the same could be true of the out-of-work chem teacher. People tend to associate termination as a black mark, an irredeemable scar that will forever brand one with the rank odor of incompetence. But a review of biographies of so many famous, accomplished people will demonstrate how many of them had to fight through a bad employment experience and often be summarily fired before they found success. Lincoln's political record is one such example. Thus, being fired can actually light a fire, turn a person in a new direction, open up a new opportunity, and be a touchpoint for the individual. How much better for the person leaving that unhappy meeting in which they receive their pink slip to find new strength; to tell their quondam boss, "Hey, you're making a mistake, but it's your mistake to make"; and to become tougher, leaner, more skilled, and more resilient as a result!

THE ROLE MODEL

"For we are naturally disposed to admire more than anything else the man who shows fortitude in adversity."[4]

In the last section, Epictetus noted that facing the Nemean lion and the rest of his monstrous menagerie built Hercules into a hero, forcing him to battle and compete and become better than he otherwise would have been. It also, though, made him a hero, causing him to be recognized by others as someone who could take it and still accomplish great things. Adopting the Stoic attitude has the real potential to do the same. The Stoic does not wail and moan when he is given an impossible task, swarmed by enemies, or fired unfairly. Rather, he accepts that life is unfair and random and that the only thing he can control is his response to outward realities, not those realities themselves. So he picks up his walking staff without a whimper and accomplishes new, impressive things. As he does so, he becomes a role model for others. He earns respect. He may even gain fame.

Is that necessarily important to a Stoic? No, It's not particularly. The Stoic does not crave the regard of others, except inasmuch as it results from something worthy he has done. Still, being respected is welcome, and if truly "we are *naturally* disposed to admire . . . the man who shows fortitude in adversity," then that person must be living according to human nature as people were designed to live, out of which comes joy and tranquility.

While not everyone will notice the efforts and success of the elementary teacher with the large, demanding classroom, her colleagues will. Her principal, no doubt, will. The students, who often know more than adults think they do, may as well—as will the parents of those students. There is little to acclaim about a teacher who handles a small class of teachers' pets. There is much to regard for the one with the classroom described above. Unfortunately, some will see in the vicious parent attacks on the middle school teacher something she, at least in part, brought on herself. But the longer she stands, the longer she calmly and professionally explains the reality of the situation to supervisors, the more she will begin to recognize the strength and character of the rock that withstands so many crashing waves. And if that chemistry teacher really does reinvent himself for some other line of work or even just finds a new school that appreciates his methods and very much appreciates his results, others will take note of that as well, and some will come to understand the nobility in being fired unfairly and not allowing it to define them.

Gratitude Rather Than Regret

But many men fail to count up how manifold their gains have been, how great their rejoicings. Grief like yours has this among other evils: it is not only useless, but thankless. Has it then all been for nothing that you have had such a friend? During so many years, amid such close associations, after such intimate communion of personal interests, has nothing been accomplished? Do you bury friendship along with a friend? And why lament having lost him, if it be no avail to have possessed him? Believe me, a great part of those we have loved, though chance has removed their persons, still abides with us. The past is ours, and there is nothing more secure for us than that which has been.[5]

As with moderns, one of the great tragedies of life for the ancients was to lose a child or close friend to death. Seneca wrote on grief at length; it was a major focus of his teachings and, as a result, of Stoicism as well. Because it is at the extreme, it is also a test case for the Stoic. Just how far can this philosophy go to bring joy and tranquility? One of the perspective changes Seneca recommended to people—while also being appropriately gentle with the tender feeling of people in grief—was to be grateful rather than regretful. When you lose a good friend, appreciate the years with the friend rather than the end of those years. He even asked the difficult question, "Would it be better that the departed had never lived in order to end grief?" If not, then the gain outweighs the loss. Or as the great twentieth-century philosopher, Dr. Seuss, supposedly encouraged, "Don't cry because it's over. Smile because it happened."

Seneca's advice in the extreme can certainly be applied—and more easily—to all those life experiences lesser than death. Faced with her seemingly overwhelming classroom, the elementary teacher can take a moment and be grateful for the last ten years, when her classes were all such dears. The middle school English teacher can take solace in the hundreds of other parents now and the thousands of parents in the past who were supportive, who saw the value in her teaching, and who backed her up because it was just and it was the best thing for their child. The chemistry teacher can smile at the memory of his past principals who believed in him and the experience his school district provided him, experience he will now use to gain his next position, whether inside or outside of education.

SUMMARY

To the Stoic, life's reversals are not the tragedies they are to others. Rather than shake their fist to heaven and ask, "Why me?," they take the more understanding approach and ask, "Why not me?" Bad things happen to everyone, and so one should neither be surprised nor outraged when they fall heavily upon their shoulders. Professional educators, of course, face their own unfortunate realities—things like large and challenging classes, impossible-to-please parents, or termination from their jobs. The difference between the Stoic educator and others, though, is in their response to them, a frequent theme for those holding firm to this philosophical school. Thus, they accept as part of professional life that bad things will come their way. They prepare for such through negative visualization, thereby taking the sting out of such events by becoming familiar with them and formulating, formally or informally, steps to take when the boom has been lowered.

They recognize that it is through tribulation that they are strengthened, that they will become better for having fought the good fight. They acknowledge that, though the regard of others is not to be valued in and of itself, being appropriately esteemed for facing down and triumphing over adversity is a positive thing and one consistent with how human nature is designed. Finally, they work hard to appreciate, to be grateful for the positives they encountered before the negative, that what came before is every bit as real as what has come now, that a loss brings pain precisely to the extent that the thing lost once brought so much joy.

NOTES

1. Epictetus, *The Enchiridion*, book 3.
2. Epictetus, *The Discourses*, book 1, chapter 24.
3. Epictetus, *The Discourses*, book 1, chapter 6.
4. Seneca, *Letter from a Stoic*, On the Shortness of Life, 13.
5. Seneca, *Letter from a Stoic*, On Consolation to the Bereaved, Letter XCIX.

Conclusion

PEOPLE TEND TO RUN INTO TWO TYPES OF PHILOSOPHY IN THEIR LIVES both in college but, possibly, elsewhere. The first is that Introduction to Philosophy, a three-credit course so many take to fulfill a humanities requirement. The curriculum for this tends toward the mind expanding, helping students to think about things in different ways or even challenging their world views and ethical systems. These are interesting and can have a long-term influence on the university freshmen, but usually what is learned there is soon cast aside as major coursework and more vocational studies take precedence. The second, limited to a much, much smaller group of students, is that of academic philosophy—the intensive studies of philosophical schools, philosophers, language, logic, and so forth. Such studies, especially when pursued into the graduate level, become increasingly, well, academic, even arcane. To the extent these have any relevance to people or society, their influences are minor and limited in most cases.

This wasn't always true. In its heyday, one that lasted arguably at least five hundred years from the rise of Zeno of Citium to the establishment of Christianity as the official religion of the Roman Empire, Stoicism was a widely held approach to life. To be clear, it was not some interesting but largely beside-the-point philosophical approach, as topics from the introductory course are treated, but it was a major—and for centuries, arguably the dominant—philosophy guiding the lives of prominent and not-so-prominent Greeks and Romans. That Marcus Aurelius was not just a practitioner but one of the great thinkers of Stoicism demonstrates its prominence.

That does not mean, however, that there were no other contenders. Founders and advocates of Epicureanism, Skepticism, and Cynicism all sallied forth in order to seize the cultural stage, and all have had continuing influences on Western civilization. Part of this was mercantile, great thinkers establishing schools in Athens and Rome and elsewhere and literally making a living by teaching students the tenets of their systems. Each of them can make a legitimate case as to the preferable way to live a life and do so without the kinds of internal contradictions or external inconsistencies with observed reality that make them obviously wrongheaded.

But Stoicism seems special. First of all, it has never entirely disappeared, and even to the extent that it has gone into intellectual hibernation for decades or centuries, it has kept popping back up, like one of those inflatable clowns that children can never seem to knock down, at least not for long—except this clown is sporting a toga. A search for Stoicism in a favorite search engine will bring up endless results.

Second, Stoicism has a canon that can be accessed *and enjoyed* by the lay reader. OK, it is not a canon that has been accepted by any governing body or that is limited to only so many documents, but it's one that has been manifested through the *Great Conversation*. The *Great Conversation* is the term Mortimer Adler and Robert Hutchins used for those books that have passed the test of time, that are read and reread by generation after generation of scholars and readers and, by the continued esteem in which they are held, proved to be worthy. They are the great books determined to be made such by the timeless conversation—literally timeless since thinkers continue to debate the notions within with those of the present and of the long past. Even death does not end the conversation. Homer is read by millions still today. The meaning of his works begins with him but is then deliberated upon by all those who read him and write about his contributions, the Iliad and the Odyssey, down the ages up until the present day. Seneca was still giving solace, as another example, to the literary consolation of Boethius, a Christian philosopher who read him in prison in the sixth century.

The Discourses and *Enchiridion of Epictetus* (even though actually written by his student Arian, which thereby began the conversation immediately, in some sense), the *Meditations of Marcus Aurelius*, and *Letters of Lucilius* by Seneca (along with scads of other writings) are all universally acclaimed as great books, and all are widely available. Because they are so and not at all painful to read, virtually anyone can join in. When they do, Stoicism influences yet another generation.

Finally, and though all philosophical schools of Greece and Rome offered the useful along with the aethereal, these Stoic masters provided to students and readers actual useful advice and techniques for applying their principles, solving life's problems, and finding joy—true, deep joy. In a world in which self-help books have been making bestseller lists since they began (i.e., more than a century ago), Stoic ideas have their appeal.

APPLYING STOICISM

For those educators and others (though this book was written specifically for those in the teaching arts) who decide there might just be something to what the emperor taught, the question becomes one of commitment. Is it better to jump on the chariot and never look back, applying Stoic thought in its entirety or to just try out one or two techniques that seem as if they might prove productive? Is it better to be purist or eclectic? Even the purist will find it difficult to really follow everything the great Stoics had to say. Their works are replete with references to the gods, Zeus at length, and it is unlikely than many readers today are believers in the Greco-Roman pantheon. (Scholars still debate if these philosophers actually believed in these gods or simply accepted them as cultural markers and their stories as useful allegories.)

But for those who believe trying a new way of thinking requires an all-out effort to, for example, give the philosophy a genuine try, either a review of the canon described above or, at least, a careful rereading of chapter 1 is in order. Doing so means accepting that joy is the summum bonum of life. It means understanding that joy is more than or different from happiness, joy being a deep-seated current of tranquility largely unaffected by daily life. It means cleaving to the idea that living life well requires one to live in accordance with nature and that nature means living as human beings were designed to live. Much of that human nature is wrapped up in social obligations, those things all people owe to one another. And it means living lives of virtue by properly understanding and living up to the four Stoic virtues: courage, wisdom, restraint, and justice. Being a Stoic is a lifetime commitment if done well. Living as a Stoic also has great rewards—joy and tranquility—as evidenced by the lives of Zeno, Epictetus, Seneca, and Marcus Aurelius.

Still, the purist approach is not mandatory. The eclectic approach is less demanding, involving taking some of the ideas or techniques of Stoicism—those that seem good and those that provide the anticipated results—and giving them a try. Thus, for example, the eclectic Stoic might latch onto negative visualization as promising. They have some crisis or controversy in their lives and wish to steele and maybe prepare themselves for the worst possible outcome. They find a quiet place and, perhaps once a day, imagine just that as vividly as they can—what happens, what others say, how they feel, and how they will respond. Then they consider just how to mentally plan for such a poor outcome. If the result is just more misery over a longer period of time for an event that never even comes to pass and this happens after several tries with varied possibilities, then negative visualization is not for them. Then again, did such attempts perhaps help them appreciate what they do have? When the worst didn't arrive, did it leave them feeling not just relieved but appreciative of the things they currently possess, which they didn't lose? If so, perhaps this technique does have something going for it.

Or what about anger control? The emperor provides ten arguments and thereby ten techniques for not getting angry. On its face, deflecting anger is a Stoic win since such internal tribulation destroys, even if only temporarily, tranquility. The eclectic Stoic can take one or more of the methods, the reinterpretation of seemingly unfortunate events, and see if it truly abates anger. If not, try some others. Or what of discarding all fretting over that which the practitioner doesn't truly control? When someone commits a hit-and-run and damages their automobile, a never-before-seen rabbit wipes out newly sprouted vegetables, or a hired painter gets the wrong address and paints the home a truly stunning lilac, why invest time or energy into an emotional response? What's done is done, and there is really nothing the Stoic could have done about any of them. There is no control, no response, no interference with tranquility;

neither, truly, is the Stoic educator's principal or superintendent or school board. If they take measures inconsistent with well-reasoned, well-researched methods, by all means, they should fight the good fight. Courage, when informed by wisdom, demands it. But what they should not do is invest that fight with anxiety or wild emotion. In the end the decision is not theirs to make, and so neither should they accept the passionate responsibility for it.

That certainly does not exhaust all of the techniques of Stoicism covered in even this small book. Such would include the following:

- Negative visualization
- Appreciation of what one has, not allowing constant grasping to detract from the present good things in life
- Living as human beings were designed to live and sticking with it
- Valuing that which should be valued
- Time is expensive; using it wisely
- Memento Mori
- Focusing only on that which can be controlled
- Dressing modestly and with utilitarian purpose
- Not allowing others to misguide or seduce one away from the legitimate purpose of a human being
- Maintaining a sense of calm and decorum
- Controlling your anger
- Understanding and accepting that bad things will happen

Selecting one and attempting to apply to life—professional or personal—is one way to take Stoicism out for a spin.

STOICISM AND THE PROFESSIONAL EDUCATOR

Stoicism does have one very relevant, particular argument in its favor for the educator. Stoics believe that finding tranquility and joy requires adherence to human nature as it is designed. And it is designed for the fulfilling of social obligations to others, to serving. What better profession to have taken up, what better vocation to have to answer the call, than education? For those who have done so, Stoicism should be given more than a glance, more than a quick read and then on to the next thing, especially if, like for so many just now, a good bit of the joy that comes from teaching has been drained away.

Having said that, the time for talk is done. Now is the time to determine whether or not adopting Stoicism, in all or in part, has promise for restoring the joy that normally is inherent in the profession and craft of education, or as the emperor has more pithily said it, "Waste no more time arguing what a good man should be. Be one."[1]

NOTE
1. Marcus Aurelius, *Meditations*, book X, chapter 16.

Appendix

Can a Christian Be a Stoic? Can an Atheist?

After reflecting a while on the principles of Stoicism, some begin to wonder how it fits in with their other worldviews, especially when they see those others as primary. After all, in the time of the ancient Stoics, Christianity either did not exist or it was a tiny sect of people who most people considered religious nuts. There is also some history involved. Stoicism waned as Christianity waxed, and while contemporaneousness—like correlation—is not causation, most historians interested in these times argue rather persuasively that Christianity rang the death knell for Stoicism as it existed in the ancient world.

Speaking of interesting nexuses, Seneca, the great Roman Stoic and financial titan, was born in the same year many believe Jesus of Nazareth was born: 4 BC. Some believe, though the evidence is far from convincing, that Pontius Pilate was a Stoic. Thus, the person who sentenced Jesus to death—or at least allowed it to happen under the sanction of his authority—may have followed the Stoic philosophy. (Then again, the question, "What is Truth?" sounds more along the lines of Skepticism or even Cynicism than Stoicism.) Finally, the author of Acts, the New Testament book immediately following the Gospels, specifically mentions the Stoics along with the Epicureans jousting with the apostle Paul in the public square in Athens. Unfortunately, little of their actual conversation or debate was recorded, and it quickly moved into one focusing almost entirely on Paul's preaching—important to Christian theology and belief but less than enlightening on more core issues of Stoicism.

All of this makes it clear that Stoicism and Christianity were both vying for the hearts and minds of men at the same time in history. That debate, that struggle, ended in Christianity being ascendant and Stoicism descendant. Did their bout, though, and its outcomes settle things for all time? Perhaps they did not. For one thing, the Roman Empire is no more. The vast expanse of Roman rule could not be held together by military might alone. (Incursions from other empires and the incursions of the barbarian hordes had proven this.) Might had to be reinforced by a shared culture. If everyone from Spain to Asia Minor, from northern Europe to northern Africa, could embrace common political, social, philosophical, and religious beliefs and practices, no external enemy could prevail against her. If they were simply an assemblage of bickering nations with widely distinct worldviews, though, no military might could hope to stand bestride her for very long, even with those incredible Roman roads.

Since few things can cohere or separate groups like religious belief, new sects were problematic. Religious freedom, as practiced by the Persians under Cyrus the Great, which allowed the Hebrews to return to their homeland, is notable because it was so rare in the ancient world. Far more common was the Roman practice of imposing the Greco-Roman pantheon, as well as emperor worship, on conquered peoples. Most conquered peoples accepted these new idols with a shrug. That the Israelites reacted with rebellion was surprising to Rome, even though local Roman officials, governors and procurators, provided clear warnings of such. Thus, Paul's visit to Athens and, later, Rome and the preaching he did there were perceived as frontier hicks failing to assimilate and stupidly making their refusal known rather than just worshiping as they saw fit in private. The philosophers in the Athenian square referred to him as a scavenger, a seed picker. In such a historical framework, when a philosophical system with religious implications met a religious system with philosophical implications, one was going to win and the other, lose.

In the contemporary West, though, freedom of religion is widely accepted. Thus, both Christianity and Stoicism can coexist indefinitely. While it is not possible to accept all facets of both systems in their entireties, there are shared understandings, and it seems reasonable to believe that a Christian could also accept many Stoic beliefs and practices.

If the purpose of Stoicism is joy and the purpose of Christianity is salvation in the hereafter, wouldn't it still be possible to be joyful in this world (the only world most Stoics accepted then and largely still today) and enjoy salvation in the next? The conflict is clear, especially inasmuch as many Christian traditions emphasize the way of the cross, the *via dolorosa*, as being a frequent companion of the adherent. Then again, Stoics acknowledge that life is sometimes difficult. They simply minimize or blot out the significance of such. Christians are more likely to embrace it. Still, Christians could pursue joy in this life—the deep, underlying joy both they and Stoics seek (though define slightly differently) while still pursuing a really happy afterlife.

The next issue at hand, though, is both systems' understandings of human nature. Stoicism argues that to be joyful, the human person must live according to nature and their human nature because that is how they were designed to live. This includes their social nature and the importance of meeting the obligations every person has to others. While Christianity largely views humanity as having a fallen-but-redeemed nature, much of their moral tradition is a matter of living consistently with natural law—that is, with how human beings are designed, as well as revealed truth. Notice, though, how they arrive in the same place. While Stoics wouldn't necessarily agree that the first commandment would be to love God, they would largely agree with loving your neighbor as yourself, at least as far as meeting basic obligations to others. There is, in other words, sufficient room for agreement that human beings—since all but the mentally ill live lives of nuance and not black-and-white demarcations—can accept the understanding of human nature for both.

VIRTUES

What then of the Stoic virtues of courage, wisdom, restraint, and justice? At first glance, they certainly look similar to the cardinal virtues accepted by various branches of Christianity. These include fortitude (akin to courage), prudence (akin to wisdom), temperance (restraint), and justice. An at-least-slight problem, though, is that superficial similarities don't necessary translate into the deep understandings of each of these virtues. Courage/fortitude, for the Stoic, means meeting obligations to others, accepting the full responsibility of human nature, and accepting truth, including rejecting untruth. For the Christian, it means living the Christian lifestyle steadfastly and publicly proclaiming the faith even unto martyrdom. (Seneca, remember, was also essentially martyred.) The courage really is the same, though it is easy to see how that courage may be directed at somewhat different intentions. The Stoic might say that accepting death rather than abandoning truth is to understand that without truth, there is no joy and that death is not to be feared in any case. The Christian would also take the martyr's crown because she will not abandon the truth, the faith, and that to do otherwise is to risk salvation. The fundamental difference is the belief in the afterlife and the effects that belief has on just what courage means. Still, courage is courage, and there is even a great deal of shared understanding between the two systems that such should be displayed.

Prudence may sound a bit different than wisdom, but remember that, for the Stoic, wisdom means knowing the difference between good and evil and detecting between that which can be controlled and that which cannot be. For the Christian, wisdom is discerning the will of God, much of which is also noting the difference between good and evil. Additionally, there is a long tradition in Christianity of Niebuhr's serenity prayer. (See chapter 1.) One illustrative example of such can be found in *The Shadow of His Wings*, a biography of a German Catholic seminarian, Gereon Goldmann, who found himself conscripted into the SS (Schutzstaffel). In a POW (prisoner of war) camp a few months before Germany's defeat, the now Father Goldmann was ministering to his flock of captured German soldiers when one of them received the news that his entire family, wife and four children, had been rolled over by a Russian tank and killed. The priest brought him the news and feared he would commit suicide. Instead, the faithful Christian only said, "Thy will be done!"[1] Such acceptance can be hard to fathom, but it does nevertheless exist.

Certainly, some Stoic wisdom would seem wrongheaded to Christians, and no doubt, the opposite is also true. For example, the admonition of Christ to turn the other cheek would seem ludicrous to a Stoic, who would certainly not see that as an obligation to others. The Christian sense of what is owed to the least of one's brothers and that providing for them is providing for another (the Son of God) would be summarily dismissed. Still, the virtue is the same. That Christianity sees wisdom where Stoicism does not is important, but the underlying reality remains.

Perhaps no greater consistency among virtues is found in the two systems than in temperance or prudence. The Stoic has identified what is essential and limits himself to it. Zeno was basically an ascetic, not necessary to but certainly consistent with temperance. The Christian seeks to restrain physical desires and live with indifference to property and wealth, as both are better used to provide for the poor and also to reduce distraction from higher things. The point of such may be different—pursuit of joy and tranquility vs. pursuit of joy and also unimaginable joy in the afterlife, but in terms of day-to-day decision making, Zeno's physical surroundings and behavior when it comes to clothing, property, food, and even illness would look a lot like that of a deeply committed Christian.

Justice, the capstone and culminating virtue of the Stoics, is also the virtue most acclaimed in Christian scriptures. It is the source and summit of all the Ten Commandments. It is also found midway through the Beatitudes, as well as at the very end. Marcus Aurelius defined it as meeting the obligation to others as well as the notion of mutual interdependence, that ensuring that all were provided for would ultimately bring joy to the one who so met those obligations.[2] Thus, these appear to be very similar. At least two important differences do exist, though. First, Christians also see strong obligations to God. Stoics recognize the importance of the gods and, for some, meeting the cultural expectations to do so, but the commitment is less intense and—given the possibility of a more superficial faith in their pantheon—even halfhearted. Second, just what constitutes a social obligation, meeting the criterion of justice, is markedly different. Stoics would view their obligation to a parent, child, sibling, or fellow citizen as quite limited, as binary. The few things the obligation requires were either met or not. To the Christian, the obligation is vastly more extensive and is never finally met. Peter asks, "How many times must I forgive my brother? Seven times?" Christ responds,

"Seven times seventy."[3] This is not equivalent to 490, but to an endless number of times. Obligations are never fully met. Debts never fully paid. The Stoic would see in that an endless disruption of tranquility. Still, the difference is one of degree, not kind. That such obligations exist is true for both. How far they extend is different.

What can be drawn from this? Differences exist, of course. To the extent, though, that they demand more of the Christian means that the lesser demanding Stoicism can be met while pursuing the more demanding. People are nuanced, and finding a way to embrace the shared meaning of these virtues as both a Christian and Stoic seems quite plausible. Even when conflict does arrive, the Christian could easily decide to pursue the Christian virtue (easily decide, *not* easily pursue) even at the expense of the meaning of the Stoic one. In some sense, this is eclectic, but in another, it is simply adding (hopefully nonsyncretically) some extra means of finding meaning in this life.

TECHNIQUES

Now, it is important to get down to the nitty-gritty. If there is room in purpose, understandings of human nature, and basic virtues between Stoicism and Christianity, what about in the Stoic techniques? It may be best to take them one at a time.

- Negative visualization: There don't seem to be any admonitions for Christians to refrain from preparing themselves for the worst. What would seem to be the case, though, would be the sources of solace for such. A lost job, a lost pet, and a lost child are all possible subjects for negative visualization—some, of course, far worse than others. Add to the Stoic's attempt to inure himself to the loss and prepare for it the Christian's sense of taking up his cross and the promise of justice and restoration in the afterlife, and it may simply be a matter of the Christian having a much fuller toolbox. The Stoic might say, though, that the Christian is failing to acknowledge the truth. Rejecting that, however, the Christian could find a richer experience with negative visualization.

- Appreciation of what one has, not allowing constant grasping to detract from the present good things in life: For Christians, the higher level of prayer is the one said out of gratitude, the *thank you* prayer. There is no conflict here. Plus, it seems an unlikely coincidence that the populations in wealthier nations experience declines in religious identification, while those of poorer nations do not.

- Live as human beings were designed to live and stick with it: Both the Stoics and Christians have a strong sense of the underlying reality of human nature. (See above.) While the two are not identical, neither are they contradictory, and so remembering to live as human beings are intended to live is not necessarily an impediment.

- Value that which should be valued: This is a matter of the purposes of human nature, the social obligations to others, and the various virtues as understood by both. The Christian's valuing is more extensive, certainly more difficult, than the Stoic's. Thus, the Christian will meet the Stoic obligations and then move past them for the seemingly endless Christian ones. The Stoic's hundred-yard dash can simply be the beginning of the Christian's marathon.

- Time is expensive, use it wisely: In some ways, this reverses the situation of *value* just above. Time is exceedingly short for the Stoic, for there is no afterlife. For the Christian, time on earth is equally short but followed by eternity. Even so, this really doesn't present much of a problem for the Christian adopting some Stoic viewpoints. Earthly life is the time and space to live the Christian life, and once done, judgment occurs. Thus, earthly time is precious, for it is the only time to demonstrate faith, virtue, and charity, as well as all of the other important aspects upon which life is judged. Thus, that there is more time is not "in play" for that judgment. Time, then, is really equally expensive for both the Stoic and the Christian, presenting no problems for the latter adopting certain aspects of the former.

- Memento mori: Remembering and reflecting upon one's personal death has different purposes for the Stoic and the Christian. The Stoic uses it as a motivation to begin living in earnest, to stop wasting time and get about the business of a fully human person. For the Christian, it is a reminder that life is short and death is long, and thus, adhering to Christian values here and now is important since judgment looms. Christians have a long tradition of memento mori. St. Jerome, who translated the scriptures into Latin, kept a human skull on his writing desk. St. Francis of Assisi carried one with him. In his Rule, the instruction to the monks of his order (and one influential in all monastic rules in the West going forward), St. Benedict explicitly directed his followers to keep death daily before their eyes. There is no reason practicing memento mori can't include both purposes.

- Focus only on that which can be controlled: This Stoic principle, while highly emphasized, especially by the emperor, is more a matter of degree. Everyone understands that it is pointless to spend time and resources on things entirely beyond one's control. OK, maybe NASA has started worrying about near earth objects (NEOs), those pesky things which have the potential to wipe out all or most life on Earth (as happened to the dinosaurs and at least a couple of other times in the planet's history), but for everyone else, the possibility of being hit by a meteorite is worth neither the effort nor the worry. There is some relevance to Christianity, though, as in the concept of scrupulosity, a defect or even sin in which the person becomes so obsessed with even the remote possibility of minuscule sins that they are unable to lead a normal life. Ministers and counselors help those suffering from such, in part, by pointing out that some things cannot be controlled. All in all, though, the notion that the uncontrollable is not to be fretted over poses no real concern for the practicing Christian.

- Dress modestly and with utilitarian purpose: No apparent conflict between this Stoic concept and Christian principles seems to exist.

- Do not allow others to misguide or seduce from the legitimate purpose of a human being: Stoicism and Christianity would share this instruction, certainly on the most obvious level. On a deeper level, there is the issue, however, of the purpose of a human being. For the Stoic, it is to find happiness, joy, and tranquility in this life, as well as to accept death without fear as something uncontrollable. For the Christian, there is a great deal more and an enormous difference in the understanding of death and what follows. When looking at the idea of a Christian-Stoic educator, though, none of these differences seem insurmountable.

- Maintain a sense of calm and decorum: While nothing in Christianity insists upon living calmly, neither does anything prohibit it.

- Control your anger: As an overall bit of counsel, Christianity would have little to say against controlling anger. But what of the emperor's ten thoughts on anger? In fact, none of them contradict Christian principles, and many have a ring of familiarity. Item one, for example, talks about the obligation people have for one another (Ten Commandments and Beatitudes), while item two asks the person tempted to be angry to try to see the whole person, not just the offense (see the child of god first, the sin second). The third emulates Christ at his crucifixion and Stephen at his martyrdom in Acts, accepting that those who give offense (sin) know not what they do. Items four, five, and seven can be summed up in the admonition "not to judge lest you be judged."[4] Items six and eight have little bearing on Christianity one way or the other.

  The ninth suggests the Stoic correct his brother in his unwise (sinful) actions but do so in sincere ways that might be effective, evoking thoughts of Christ's encouragement in the Gospel of Matthew to correct one's brother in order to turn him away from his inappropriate behavior and thereby win back that brother. The Book of James has an even stronger lesson in this regard, arguing that doing so garners significant benefits for the one intervening (covering a multitude of sins), though this book is not accepted as

canonical by some denominations. Finally, item ten will be familiar to the Christian, as it reflects humanity's fallen nature.

A Stoic's call then to control anger, in its arguments for doing
so, will be familiar to the practicing Christian and should present
no impediments to this philosophy.

- Understand and accept that bad Things will happen: To what
Christians might describe as a fallen nature or fallen world, the
Stoics would offer little dissent. The story of the Fall from Genesis
would not necessarily ring true, of course, but inasmuch as that
story results in a nature that everyone must face, the Stoics would
see the value in it. It all comes to the same—a world in which
difficult things happen and struggles become necessary. To expect
otherwise is nonsensical.

SUMMARY: STOICISM AND CHRISTIANITY
Though there are clearly differences between certain aspects of the purpose, understanding of nature (human and otherwise), core virtues, and
certain practices of Stoicism and Christianity, it remains true, nonetheless, that there is little or nothing to prevent a Christian from adopting
much of the Stoic philosophy and pretty much all of the Stoic practices.
(Compare this to Marxism, for example, which essentially requires atheism, and the nature of any obstacles can be seen with a softer eye.) Still,
though, is this philosophy such an intellectual edifice that taking it on
would detract from an earnest Christian's pursuit of that guiding light?

This is not necessarily the case. While syncretism (the uncriti-
cal adoption of parts of various religious, philosophical, or cultural concepts
into an amalgam that leaves the believer with an unsatisfactory mish-
mash divorced from its original sources and containing unaddressed
contradictions) should be avoided, it is also true that religions pick up
cultural and other aspects as they develop and gather additional adher-
ents. The challenge, in fact, for many religions is safeguarding its core
beliefs while remaining open to other developments that enhance it and
allow it to adapt to or address a changing world. Thus, for example, early
Christianity adopted a Platonist (arguably Neoplatonist) view of science

and human understanding. As that became increasingly untenable, it was Thomas Aquinas who is said to have baptized Aristotle, thereby allowing Christendom to accept the Aristotelian view of science.

They key to accepting such developments is not doing so when such would destroy the core beliefs of a religious faith. Since Stoicism does not do so, as long as the Greco-Roman pantheon can be thrown out and certain other reinterpretations (central values, practices such as memento mori, etc.) made, the modern Christian would not seem to be logically prevented from integrating much of Stoic philosophy.

WHAT, THEN, OF ATHEISM?

A similar analysis of atheism is possible. In doing so, it is important to keep in mind that, like Christianity's many denominations, atheism also has any number of intellectual sects. The shared core belief—an absence of God—is accompanied by many tendencies, including a belief in the scientific method, but they will vary with the adherent. Thus, this analysis is an attempt to look broadly at a general notion of atheism and will, thus, invariably miss certain aspects because of the variety in this area.

The review begins, again, with purpose. The Stoic pursuit of a joyful life does not fully capture the atheist viewpoint in all its possible permutations, but an atheist who did pursue a happy life would not be a contradiction. A recent Pew survey of atheists and the source of their meaning in life mentioned any number of things, though none of them included meeting social obligations. Still, this had more to do with the survey's construction than any atheist stance toward such since its foils were close-ended rather than open-ended. Many atheists are, indeed, humanists (an atheist need not be a humanist, nor must a humanist be an atheist), which would then orient them towards meeting social obligations and serving others. It is reasonable to argue that an atheist who had humanist tendencies and saw helping others as a major aspect of their life could adopt a Stoic outlook without much angst. That is not to say it would orient them toward Stoicism, though—simply, that the two would not be internally inconsistent.

Neither, necessarily, would a view of human nature be inconsistent. Certainly, the general Stoic view that human nature is simply how the gods designed it as emanating from nature generally is a problem for the atheist, but it's hardly an insurmountable one. By simply replacing such design with evolution by natural selection (or one of its increasingly technical tweaks), the atheist can accept the social nature of humanity. Because human beings descended from primates, likely earlier forms than exist today, and because primates are social creatures—their social organization providing them with certain survival advantages in prehistorical times and still today—they have a nature that brings positive outcomes from meeting obligations to others in the group. It is no wonder then that meeting such obligations provides underlying joy and tranquility. The cause, the source, of human nature and its realities is not the same, but they arrive at the same point, nonetheless. This is very much consistent with reasonable developments of systems of thought. Atheism—or better, certain atheists—accepts the primary reality of meeting social obligations to others, even though they view it as arising from a different source. All systems of thought that "intend" to survive must develop over time, and this development poses no threat to atheism's larger beliefs— that is, the lack of a god or gods.

VIRTUES

What, then, of the four cultural values of Stoicism: courage, wisdom, restraint, and justice? Once again, humanism would have more to say here than atheism since the latter only cleaves to one overall belief. Some arguments could be made for each, nevertheless. Stoic courage, unflinchingly facing the unvarnished truth, is very much a source of pride among atheists. While others, they argue, fool themselves with beliefs in a god or gods, they wave off that unnecessary concept and face a reality without such a creator, lawgiver, or judge. They take what they view as their courageous position in a largely unsympathetic world.

Stoic wisdom is a bit tougher. Identifying the difference between good and evil is often a utilitarian calculus—is there a benefit and for how much, for how many?—but is possible and, in the atheist's view, necessary since divine law is nonsense. Atheists can easily split on that which is controllable and that which is uncontrollable, with many accepting a deterministic world with no free will (though some still argue the best results come when free will still underlies decision making). Determinism makes wisdom easy; that is, nothing is ultimately controllable. This doesn't obviate Stoicism, but it does make this important observation and advice of Stoics—ignore that which is outside of one's control—meaningless. The nondeterminist atheist, who allows at least some form of free will, could still find this aspect of Stoic wisdom valuable.

Stoic restraint, limiting oneself to that which is essential, could be all over the board for atheists. If an atheist found a spartan lifestyle a happy one or even just a useful one, nothing in atheism prevents that pursuit. If an atheist found a life of comparative excess, though, joyful or utilitarian, nothing in atheism prevents that either. Thus, the individual atheist would find this core Stoic value a positive or not, i.e., their individual call.

Stoic justice, for Marcus Aurelius at least, inheres in mutual interdependence, living a life in connection with others and ensuring that one's individual life does not detract—and hopefully enhances—the lives of all others, especially those in close proximity, but even all other human beings. As with restraint, this depends upon the individual atheist. Those who tend toward humanism will definitely be on board with Stoic justice, at least in intent. Others may not see this as relevant, simply assuming that social structures—capitalism, political realities, and so forth—are positive or negative but, ultimately, beyond the means of any individual to really impact. Thus, atheists will pursue or not pursue the Stoic sense of justice as they see fit. Certainly, though, they can adopt this Stoic idea, and even if they don't, they can still adopt other aspects of the philosophy without it.

TECHNIQUES
What remains, then, are the following techniques:

- Negative visualization: The idea of preparing oneself for both the emotional reality of an unfortunate outcome and for a productive response, could be useful to the atheist as much as any other. It would be an odd belief for an atheist to hold that somehow bad things would not occur in his life. No one is watching over him, no one protecting him, other than himself and those in his life who support him. Thus, negative visualization could be practiced by an atheist without contradicting his core belief structure.

- Appreciation of what one has, not allowing constant grasping to detract from the present good things in life: There is some sense in atheism and the belief that "This is all there is"—that is, the lack of an afterlife—that is motivating to one to live life for all it's worth, to not accept, for example, poverty in hopes of paradise later. None of this, though, is incumbent upon atheism. Regardless, being appreciative of what one has is certainly no necessary problem for atheism, and so it's no obstacle for an atheist adopting Stoicism.

- Live as human beings were designed to live and stick with it: Atheists can adopt any range of ideas on how human beings are designed to live, if they even accept the strictures that life is designed in the first place. Adopting this Stoic technique, for the atheist, then might mean deciding just what that design is, in general or for the individual. As long as the "designed" lifestyle selected by the atheist is consistent with a lack of a belief in a god, committing to how life is to be lived would pose no problem for the atheist's wish to utilize this Stoic technique.

- Value that which should be valued: Without a belief in a god or a system of value that would logically result, the atheist might consider himself radically free to make decisions about that which should be valued and even change those values over time. As long as he valued behaviorally what he valued mentally, an atheist could follow this practice as well as any. Without an external guide—a creed, statement of priorities, and so forth—as to that value, though, it is also possible that the atheist might be more likely and willing to simply shift that which should be valued at any point, sacrificing the import of this technique. That this could happen, though, doesn't mean it must happen. Thus, an atheist could, upon sober reflection, settle upon that which should be valued and stick with it, making atheism no block for Stoicism.

- Time is expensive: With no afterlife and a pretty clearly defined time span (120 years seems to be at the very outer limit these days), the atheist should already have pretty strong buy-in with the value of time. That which cannot be done in this life cannot be done. This should be motivating, and so the atheist might very well already find himself in league with Stoicism up front.

- Memento mori: For the Stoic, death is a simple reality and a motivation to get about the business of living a fully human life. This would be no different for the atheist and so pose no problem for the adoption of this philosophical school by one.

- Focus only on that which can be controlled: This has already been sufficiently covered above, under the discussion of the core Stoic value of wisdom.

- Dress modestly and with utilitarian purpose: Some atheists would agree with this, while others would not. Those who agree could feel at home with this technique. Those who do not agree could simply discard it as part of the Stoic school apart from its more core principles. Doing so would be a small eclectic maneuver but hardly a serious rejection of the overall philosophy.

- Do not allow others to misguide or seduce from the legitimate purpose of a human being: This is an area on which many atheists pride themselves. They feel they have faced one of the ultimate realities of existence, the lack of a divine creator, and, instead of engaging in self-delusion, have stood firm. Moreover, in a world where their viewpoint is widely challenged—in part, some argue, because it threatens that self-delusion of others—they have not allowed themselves to be dissuaded from it. Popular culture, from basically as long as atheism has been understood to exist, has included scores of stories about deathbed conversions of atheists to one form or theism or another. Christians and others tell of such persons repenting of their unbelief when faced with their impending death. In World War II, this reality was expressed with the saying, "There are no atheists in fox holes." In more modern times, stories have circulated that atheist-evangelist Christopher

Hitchens and scientist Stephen Hawking repented of their disbelief at the end, the latter being persuaded to do so by none other than Pope Francis himself, but atheists roundly dispute such, and little evidence points to this having happened, in any case. Websites devoted to atheism roundly condemn such stories in part because they detract from this technique, not allowing one to be dissuaded from their understanding of human existence. Properly understood, then, this Stoic notion poses no issue for the atheist.

- Maintain a sense of calm and decorum: Nothing in atheism would prevent the adoption of this Stoic technique.

- Control your anger: Nothing in atheism defies anger control as a technique either. However, as with Christianity, the emperor's ten ideas related to anger are probably worth a look. Item one relates to the social nature of humanity. Assuming this social nature of humanity, emanating from evolution by natural selection and the comparative reproductive and survival advantages of human cooperation and gregariousness, an atheist can agree here. In items two and three, seeing humanity with all its foibles, through a clear lens, and understanding the ignorance in which much of humanity is steeped, the atheist may have no issues with these sources of inappropriate anger either. Items four, five, and seven, relating to the inadvisability of making judgments on others, are not necessarily principles or logical consequences of atheism but neither are they impediments to it. Thus, an atheist could certainly adopt these if it helped him along the way to joy and tranquility, without necessarily violating his belief structure. Item six, advocating for the remission of anger because life is so short, is an interesting one. Would righteous anger be obviated or energized by the atheist's view that life is fleeting and then completely, unequivocally ended? Even in the latter case, though, this is just one argument against anger. Additionally, Christopher Hitchens aside, it is possible to advocate for change without anger. Eight is such a practical maxim, with anger frequently causing more problems than the issue from which is sprang, so it would be hard to see how it could pose a problem for the atheist. Item nine, the idea that, as a part of obligations to others, the Stoic should correct others when necessary but do so in such ways—gently, genuinely, and without guile or sarcasm—is not much of a consistent factor for atheists. While some atheists definitely feel it to be important to remove the cloud of ignorance that is theism from so much of the world (Hitchens again[5]), others are fine with nonatheists finding their own way as they see fit. As a result, the atheist can give or take this argument about anger. Finally, item ten, that anger is misguided because humanity is simply irrational, is certainly within the purview of atheism. The only impediment, in fact, is with the emperor's actual statement that references Apollo and the muses—to them, an at-least-annoying aspect of his writing.

- Understand and accept that bad things will happen: That realization should be as evident to the atheist as it is to the Christian and the Stoic. Fully integrating it as a means of not allowing tragedies, mishaps, and annoyances to drain away joy would seem as attainable or as difficult to attain for the atheist as for the Stoic.

SUMMARY: STOICISM AND ATHEISM

Atheism's limited scope, a singular lack of belief in a god or gods, leaves it very amenable to other concepts without logical inconsistencies. While its purpose and sense of human nature is not identical to those of Stoicism, neither do they necessarily conflict. Thus, an atheist can accept joy as the purpose of life and a social human nature, including the obligations to others as preferred candidates. While an "unbeliever" will have certain proclivities in interpreting and prioritizing the aspects of the Stoic core values, none of them pose an insurmountable obstacle to adopting Stoicism as a philosophy of life or adopting any number of aspects of it. As to the Stoic techniques or practices discussed in this work, again, an atheist would be unevenly disposed toward some of them over others. Some they would take in a different direction than others, especially those involving time, death, and the afterlife, but all can be accepted and utilized (without too much intellectual juggling). Thus, in general, there is nothing to prevent the atheist from adopting the Stoic philosophical perspective.

This is important, at least at present, because atheism is currently on the rise. K–12 educators, particularly at the high school level but increasingly at any level, are taking note of a growing separation of students from faith communities, students who are even actively espousing a lack of belief in any sort of creator. Thus, while Christianity remains the norm, atheism is currently ascendant and so is relevant to Stoicism's adoption, though it may again ebb just as it now flows.

NOTES

1. *New American Bible*, Matthew 6: 10.
2. Marcus Aurelius, *Meditations*, book XI, chapter 20.
3. *New American Bible*, Matthew 18: 21–22.
4. *New American Bible*, Matthew 7: 1–2.
5. Hitchens, *God Is Not Great*, 2007, pp. 1–13.

References

Arrrian, "Arrian to Lucius Fellius: Wisheth all Happiness," In *Moral Discourses of Epictetus*, Everyman's Library 404. United Kingdom: Dent. 1955.

Aurelius, Marcus. *Meditations* (Rome, 161–180 CE; Project Gutenberg, June 1, 2001). https://www.gutenberg.org/ebooks/2680.

Berra, Yogi, https://www.baseballbible.net/yogi-berra-quotes/.

Epictetus. *The Enchiridion* (125 CE; Project Gutenberg, March 10, 2014). https://www.gutenberg.org/files/45109/45109-h/45109-h.htm.

Epictetus. *The Moral Discourses of Epictetus*. United Kingdom: Dent, 1910.

Fast Times at Ridgemont High. Directed by Amy Heckerling, performances by Sean Penn, Jennifer Jason Leigh, Judge Reinhold, Pheobe Cates, Brian Backer, Robert Romanus, Ray Walston, Amanda Wyss, Scott Thompson, Ben Stein, and Vincent Schiavelli, Universal Pictures, 1982.

Hitchens, Christopher. *God Is Not Great: How Religion Poisons Everything*. United Kingdom: Twelve, 2007.

Johnson, Samuel. *The Life of Boswell*. London: Penguin Group, 2008.

Kipling, Rudyard. "If- by Rudyard Kipling." Poetry Foundation. Poetry Foundation. https://www.poetryfoundation.org/poems/46473/if———.

Niebuhr, Reinhold. Serenity Prayer, https://proactive12steps.com/serenity-prayer/, 1926.

Rufus, Musonius. *That One Should Disdain Hardships*. New Haven: Yale University Press, 2020.

Seneca, Lucius Annaeus. *Letters from a Stoic*. United Kingdom: Penguin Books, Limited, 2004.

Seneca, Lucius Annaeus. *Moral Essays*. United Kingdom: W. Heinemann, Limited, 1928.

Seneca, *The Tragedies of Seneca*, Chicago: The University of Chicago Press, 1907.

Van Loon, Hendrik Willem, *The Story of Mankind*. Liveright Publishing Corp., 1951.

Ward, Geoffrey. *The Civil War—An Illustrated History*. Knopf, 1990.

About the Author

Joseph Graves is the Secretary of Education for the State of South Dakota. Prior to that, he served as superintendent of schools in Mitchell, South Dakota for more than twenty years. He has been a superintendent, principal, and teacher for the last thirty-seven years. In addition to education and the social studies, which he taught, he also studied philosophy as both an undergraduate and a graduate student. He turned away from academic philosophy in graduate school but has read widely in the field ever since.

Like most educators, he failed to appreciate in advance the full negative impact of the COVID-19 epidemic on students, teachers, and schools. When the disastrous consequences arrived, he turned to philosophy in general—and the Stoics in particular—for a means of perspective, relief, and solution. The result is this book.

Graves divides his time between Pierre, SD, and Mitchell. He and his wife, Cheryl, have four children and ten grandchildren, about whom he is anything but stoic. He is a permanent deacon of the Roman Catholic Church. As superintendent, he wrote a semi-weekly column for the local newspaper, the Mitchell *Daily Republic.* The articles always touched on education and frequently seemed to stray into topics philosophic.